Nuggets of Gold
in Pitchers of Silver

Nuggets of Gold in Pitchers of Silver

Poetical Expressions of a Soul

Mabel Katherine Black

Guardian BOOKS

Belleville, Ontario, Canada

Poetry by Mabel Black

In Partnership with the

Holy Spirit Unlimited

Nuggets of Gold in Pitchers of Silver

Copyright © 1999, Mabel Katherine Black

ISBN: 1-55306-040-7

**For more information or
to order additional copies, please contact:**

Marjorie Johnston
69 Godstone Rd. #126,
Toronto, ON M2J 3C8

Printed in Canada
by
Guardian BOOKS

Foreword

"Out of the abundance of the heart, the mouth speaketh."
Matthew 12:34

This book *"Nuggets of Gold in Pitchers of Silver"* is truly a delightful expression of a delightful lady. In the years that I have known Mabel Black, I have been impressed over and over again by her intense love for Jesus and dedication to His work here on Earth. I've also been amazed by her joy, her vivacious love of life, her wit, and her incredible poetic talent. Mabel is an inspiration!

As you read the title of this book, you are enticed into its pages. As Mabel shares her "nuggets of gold", you will be inspired to love Jesus and to appreciate the little things in life more and more.

Life's everyday experiences are often treasures we miss. Mabel has captured them in a very refreshing and often humorous way, to preserve them and reflect their true value. Your spirit will be uplifted and your faith strengthened as you enjoy *"Nuggets of Gold in Pitchers of Silver"*.

Pastor Paul Yuke
Covenant Christian Church
455 Huron Street
Toronto, Ontario

i

Dedication

To my daughter, Marjorie Johnston. I cannot adequately express my appreciation, but I'm believing Father to abundantly bless her.

Table of Contents

iv

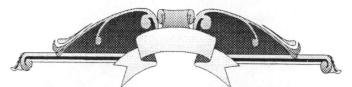

Nuggets of Gold in Pitchers of Silver

In the Bible, gold symbolizes Jehovah Yahweh God.
Silver is redemption through His precious blood.
The omnipotent Spirit and His Holy Word,
Will make us acceptable in the Beloved. 1

Jesus said: 'The old and the new would not agree.' 2
Man's sinful heart could not bear His equity.
To have His gold in our transformed soul,
We must be submissive to His control.

A longing within makes us want to be like Him,
Then He'll remove from us our dross and tin.
To Father He'll present His Bride without stain.
Together with Him for eternity, we'll reign.

---

1. Ephesians 1:6 KJV
"To the praise of the glory of His grace, wherein
He hath made us accepted in the Beloved."

2. Luke 5: 36-38 AMP
"He told them a proverb also: No one puts a patch
from a new garment on an old garment; if he does,
he will both tear the new one, and the patch from
the new one will not match the old garment. And no
one pours new wine into old wineskins; if he does,
the fresh wine will burst the skins and it will be
spilled and the skins will be ruined, destroyed.
But new wine must be put into fresh wineskins."

Introduction

I enjoy writing poetry because I feel the Holy Spirit is my Partner. I never know the end of the poem at the beginning because it comes from my spirit, not from my head. This ministry has been something that has taken place in recent years. At times I have awakened early in the morning and a poem would start coming to me. If I don't write it down when it comes, it doesn't come back. I would know who it would be for, and often a scripture would come that would encourage them in a hard place.

I'd like to share an interesting story in connection with one of my poems. Early one morning I was thinking about an experience I had when I was 23. I went downstairs to do the laundry, and I prayed a little prayer: 'Lord, what should I call my poem? The answer came right back: *'Blow off where it pays off.'* I laughed and told the Lord that I loved His humour. I finished my laundry and when I went back to my room I'd forgotten the title that He gave me. I prayed again: 'Lord, what was that funny title You gave me for my poem?' Back it came, *'Blow off where it pays off.'* That poem has blessed a lot of people.

Sometimes a title will come, then some time later, I'll get the poem. These poems are centred around experiences, testimonies, and scripture verses. A scripture verse burns in my spirit, and a poem releases it. When I don't have a pulpit to release the burden, the poem I get shares my burden.

One time I was asked to minister in a Baptist church in Haileybury, and the Pastor introduced me as a poetical evangelist ...

A Poetical Evangelist

I feel a message coming up in me
Which I love expressing in poetry.
When I start a poem, I have no goal.
It comes not from my head but from my soul.

Its like a road over which I have not been,
So the end of it I have not seen.
I can't tell what I'm going to say;
It comes line by line in a poetical way.

Its a language hidden deep in my soul.
I love it when it takes control.
The most thrilling experience to me
Is when the Lord answers in poetry.

I get a new poem most every day.
That encourages me in a beautiful way.
It is giving me a longing that is deep within --
Just to see Jesus, and be cleansed from all sin.

These poems bless me. They are from God,
And give me an intimacy with my lovely Lord.
I know they will also be a blessing to you,
And flood you with joy, as His will you do.

1

My Commitment

Lord make my consecration to You complete
So Your presence to me becomes more sweet;
That my thoughts, words, actions and ways
Shall bring to Thee glory and praise.

Cleansed, sanctified; by Your blood, nigh;
My life seasoned from fragrance on high.
May my work, my money, and all that I do
Be to bring pleasure especially to You.

Grant me an understanding heart to realize
Being a blessing to others wins the greatest prize.
I appreciate your faithful intercession for me;
Give me of that Spirit that operates strongly in Thee.

To be a blessing to others is of the same degree
That I experience our union, in reality.
Your precious blood makes all this possible
But to enter it, takes drawing from Thee.

Grant this vessel to be cleansed clear through,
According to the good pleasure designed by You.
Deal with the tarnish that hinders our connection,
Bring forth in this gold, Your own reflection.

I will hide Thy word deep in my heart,
So the right word comes forth for every dart.
I shall be strong to face the storm --
Your mighty promises in me, You will perform.

Job asked: "Is it good that He should search you out?"
Yes, it is very good. I agree with David: "Search me, O God
and know my heart: try me, and know my thoughts."

(Job 13:9; Psalms 139:23)

Lack in Me

I never had a father with whom I could be intimate.
My marriage relationship lacked love, unity and fulfilment.
My mother loved her children and suffered poverty and pain;
She was hard working, but little appreciation did gain.

I was saved when I was twelve and great joy I received.
My life was immediately changed when I believed.
Many and varied were the experiences I went through.
I did a lot of things, that now I wouldn't do.

The wrongs I did are under His precious blood;
And to uncover them would be an insult to God.
Dear Lord, I appreciate You. You're like a mother to me;
Great misery and pain, you endured to set me free.

You are so forgiving and sweet and comforting too,
But I don't feel towards Father, like I do towards You.
I repent and ask You, my heart to fill
With Your loving desire to do Father's will.

I know Father loves me and at a great, great cost
Gave His beloved for me, to the awful death of the cross.
He is not the Father to holy angels, yet He is to fallen man.
My spirit needs a revelation of this truth to understand.

I want to be like You in loving oneness with the Father.
My whole being captured with this consuming desire.
Doing His perfect will was Your constant concern,
Now may a like covenant in me deeply burn.

And Your great joy whereby You endured the cross;
Make it my joy and rejoicing, and be cleansed from all dross.
I know I shall receive it because it is Father's will,
And what You have designed for me, He shall fulfil.

I'm so grateful for the happiness, deep inside,
And for the longing You gave me to be Your spotless Bride.
There is little of my life left, but I give You the right,
In this great visitation, to make me Your delight.

In Your compassion, to minister,
Producing fruit for Your honour,
What You are, to be lived out in me
To glorify You to the fullest degree.

May Your love, like a river flow
And be manifested wherever I go.
Most of all, I want to come
To be with You in Your heavenly home.

Unveiling My Heart to Jesus

I'm not happy with the race I have run,
Or satisfied with what I have done.
I'm challenged by Leonard Ravinhill's decree,
And I know the Lord can accomplish it in me:
'I pledge from this day to the grave
To be Thine own unquestioning slave.'

John Hyde prophesied a divine restoration in 1901.
1000 years later we are witnessing it being done.
God is on the move and we don't want to miss it
Being sidetracked, or misled by the wrong spirit.
Love, wisdom, discernment and revelation, we need
To fulfill this prophesy Brother Hyde has decreed.

Lord Jesus, I need a clear understanding
What the end time, of me is demanding.
I know my heart cry is reaching Thee:
To consume me with the blaze of Your purity,
And my will be absorbed in Father's will,
Then Your oneness in me You can fulfill.

Things not seen are more real than what I'm seeing;
Situations are more real than what I'm hearing and feeling.
May my spirit be utterly controlled by God,
Be led, protected and instructed by His word.
Above all not to shrink from paying the price
To give my body to this reasonable sacrifice.

Romans 12:1

I need this deluge of your glory
To finish Salvation's love story.
Joy shall fill me to the very core.
I'll hunger for Jesus more and more.
He will send an overflowing abundance,
But flesh cannot stand such a performance.

The crucified life is not a quick fix.
The trials we face prepare us for it.
Do I really want this cleansing revival,
This anointing to finish what is eternal:
To be flushed out of all not built upon the Lord,
Open for the cleansing by the washing of His word.

In Mark 5:19 and 20, fearfully they sent Jesus away
But wanted Him back and began to repent and pray.
Jesus came back and gave them a famed deliverance,
Manifesting His love and compassion in abundance.
The whole city then changed their thinking
When from His fountain they began drinking.

There'll be many who bow and back out.
Deaf to what the Spirit is talking about.
When God uses people of lower degree,
Angrily they'll say, 'He should have used me'.
Come Lord, consume me with Your holy flame
And burn up my dross, in Your worthy name.

Then the world will know I am like You
When I do Your work like You would do.
I hear Him -- He is now passing by
To hear my response and my heart cry.
A magnet is in my spirit and it is drawing
Me to Him. His purpose He is fulfilling.

5

A Trip Down Memory Lane

There is a package of flesh hiding in me.
It is full of deceit and iniquity
Because Satan planted in it his evil nature
Then commissioned demons to make it mature.

No one taught me to lie, be greedy, or fly off the handle,
Say bad words, do bad things, verging on scandal.
Even though I stuttered and found it hard to talk,
A bad spirit was working in me before I could walk.

When I was five I could see
Demons coming in the window after me.
I was afraid and had great fear.
I told no one, lest they think I was queer.

When I was six I became very ill.
Mother sent me to Grandma to make me well.
The change of food my strength did quicken.
Then I was able to start kindergarten.

Grampa said: Few went to Heaven but many went to Hell.
I knew I would go there. I knew it well.
If I burned my finger, how horrible it would be
When I burned all over in Hell for eternity.

Very difficult situations our family faced --
Not much to eat and we were poorly dressed.
Two young ladies from the Shantymen came.
They preached the Gospel, simple and plain.

"Now who would like to invite Jesus to come in
To your heart, and cleanse it from sin?
Then love, joy, and peace shall be given,
And your name written in the Book of Life in Heaven."

I shot my hand up real high so they could see
I wanted what they said most earnestly.
They prayed with me. I felt my sin go.
I was very happy, and I told them so.

"Now will you testify for Jesus tonight?"
I know He washed my black heart white.
I was so happy then, I felt I could preach and pray.
I thought when I grew up I'd be a missionary.

I'm old now and my hair is turning white.
I've missed my Lord many times, not doing right.
He was so gracious, kind, and loving;
Many times He saved me from dying.

My wonderful Jesus, You are my Lord.
Let Father's love through me be poured.
May Your compassion emanate from my soul.
I'm so old now, but please take control.

I must know You, Lord, in a deeper way.
The needs are so many, to meet every day.
The greatness of my Lord, I must experience.
To bring to dying souls, Your deliverance.

I can't look at the size of my offering.
I must see the size of my God
Who is able in the least of His servants
To perform the same works as my Lord.

Search me precious Holy Spirit.
Show me the things I don't see.
I long for a clean wine-skin, Jesus,
One that is filled only with Thee.

I'm so happy, and I know there shall be
A performance of Your will and purpose in me.
I long to see You, Jesus, and look upon Your face
And be a trophy for Your glory, a product of Your grace.

———————— •••●●●••• ————————

I'm Getting Married Again

I am so happy and full of glee,
Something so good is coming to me.
It is thrilling as thrilling can be --
I'm getting married again, you see.
The first time through was a washout,
Filled with heartache and grave doubt.
Its different now -- no more pain.
I'm happy that I'm getting married again.
We've dated and courted many a day.
Now I'll be with Him forever to stay.

One time I felt my Lover had gone.
I was very down, and felt so alone.
My heart was sick and I couldn't pray.
Satan said: 'He wouldn't hear anyway.'
Suddenly, I did hear His sweet voice!
Darkness fled, and my heart did rejoice.
What He said was shocking to hear:
"The greatest tests, in glory will be most dear."
Really then, I'll thank You for what I'm feeling
Because I love to receive Your rich blessing.

'Lord, I want Rhoda to come.' was my prayer.
The car came, and He said: "She's not there."
I was so disappointed, I wanted to cry.
He answered so sweetly, and told me why:
"I know you wanted her, and you feel alone
But it wasn't My will for her to come."
Forgive me Lord, for being depressed.
Even if it hurts, I know Your ways are best.
Thank You for meeting me when I was undone.
I know that is the time You love to come.

8

He is making me a gown that is uniquely mine,
Adorned with jewels and needle work so fine.
A beautiful crown He will place on my brow.
I never was beautiful, but I will be now.
He knows how to fit me in perfectly.
There'll be no more flesh to bother me.
Let us rejoice over what Jesus has done.
Be jubilant over the wedding so soon to come.
It's the most glorious group to be in.
The qualification is to be one with Him.

Peace in the Midst of the Storm

We were in a large city named Hankow
And a message came that furrowed our brow.
It said, "The river's so high, just 3 more inches to go
And the weakened dike will soon overflow!"
There was nowhere to go and we stood in the door
As a strong wind came with such a loud roar!
The people panicked and were in great despair
While their wares and their goods flew everywhere.
A sister said, "I've just got a good word --
Let's praise our God and trust in the Lord.
'Hitherto shall thy proud waves come but no further.'
I know this word has come from our Heavenly Father."
We praised the Lord for His wonderful care,
His comforting peace replaced our despair.
The wind suddenly stopped -- the dike didn't break!
The God they knew not, did undertake.
The floods went down; the land was spared,
And the reason why, we happily shared.
God's gospel of peace, many were now ready to receive;
To repent of their sins, and in His word believe.

A Song for Satan

You are not in my hip, you are under my heel.
That is the fact, not the symptoms I feel.
Remember the scene at the whipping post,
When my Lord was lashed by your evil host.
How your heart filled with wicked pride
When Jesus of Nazareth you crucified.

The world was shocked as victory you won --
Their eyes being closed to the outcome.
In Hell your hosts had a different look:
Jesus, the keys of death and Hell He took.
You have lost all rights you hold on me.
Through the blood, from bondage, I'm free!

You are not in my hip, but under my heel.
I obtained it by faith -- and not by feel.
The blood ever speaks to Father for me --
My great intercessor is praying effectively.
He told me in His word, like Him I could be.
In His powerful blood, I demand you to flee!

Satan's Adjournment

Jesus said it. It's true I know:
By faith I declare it, and Satan will go.
The name of Jesus has been given to me,
And Satan knows he will have to flee.

10

Is God Listening?

I am happy to declare from my experience that
God is a prayer-answering God.
His name is Jehovah Yahweh, the Almighty God.
It is as impossible for Him to lie,
As it is for Satan to tell the truth.
If we believe God's word, we'll know
He is bigger than our circumstances...

There it was again, the third time my name was called:
"Su-Chaio-Shir, you have got to come!"
I was in panic. I was sick, weak, and deathly afraid --
Coward all the way through. I didn't want to go.
I wanted to hide. I was to be questioned,
And be at the mercy of that group of communists
About which I had heard so much.
There was no escape -- I had to go.

I took one last look at my room.
My eyes caught a glimpse of a plaque that I had made:
'In what time I am afraid, I will trust and not be afraid'.
I said: "Lord! That is now. I've never been so scared.
I believe You! Please help me!"
The situation did not change -- I still had to go,
But something changed in me. The mighty God had spoken:
"Fear not, for I am with thee."

Just as the tumultuous waves of Galilee Sea
Were instantly stilled by the voice of Jesus,
So was the tumult of my soul instantly stilled by peace.
Fear was gone! God had spoken and I believed His word.
I knew He was with me and He was in charge.
In the midst of the interrogation, suddenly the door opened:
Someone shouted something in Chinese.
The room emptied. One said on their way out:
"Tell those girls to be gone before we come back
Or it will be too bad for them."
We had been cut off in the interior of China.
We had no money and no way, but God made a way for us.

I'm not saying there were no difficulties,
But through those hard spots,
I got to know Jesus better and to appreciate Him more.
We went through one of the worst battles in Honnan.
I heard bullets whistle past my ears, but I didn't stop any.
It is the one that you don't hear that does the damage.
There were times that my life could have been taken,
But God in His mercy closed the door.

That was fifty years ago. Now, more than ever,
I believe that God will do what He says He will do.
If we believe that, we will walk in victory and not in defeat.
There is more in the Word about these very days
In which we now live than any other period in history.
We need to know what God is saying and carefully obey,
To be worthy to be hid in the great day of the Lord's wrath.
There is no escape for those who know not God.
Those who trust in God and obediently listen,
They shall be glad and exceedingly rejoice,
And great shall be their eternal reward.

I broke my hip. My doctor said: "It's a bad, bad break.
Your bones are in such poor condition,
I doubt if you will be able to walk again."
I said: "Doctor, there are a lot of gods in the world
But the One I serve is a prayer-answering God.
That leg will walk again!" That leg is walking again.
Praise His name. My wonderful Lord
Still answers prayer according to His Word.
He is a great Finisher.
Not one word He has spoken shall fail.

*'Time is a revealer
of facts and figures'.*

"Never let adversity get you down --
Only on your knees.   Romans 8:38, 39

12

The Eventful Day of Marjorie Kaye

My youngest daughter's name is Marjorie Kaye.
She wants a poem of the events that fill her day.
She comes into my room; she is still half awake,
Does exercises, puts in her contacts and a shower will take.
She rubs my feet, legs, back and knee
And a few other chores for dear broken hipped me.
She feeds the cat, the bird, and mama squirrel waits to see
If Marge will remember the nuts for her family.
She prepares salads, and my breakfast and lunch too
And awakens Rochelle which is not easy to do.
She hurriedly dresses and dawns on her coat
And rushes out of the house at 6:30 or there about.

She is on time for the big day's work yet to do,
But her body is telling her she should be half through.
She greets her buddies and gives them a smile
Then sinks into her chair to rest for awhile.
The phone rings. She answers 'Yes, yes. That I'll do.
As soon as I get the information, I'll get back to you.'
So information to get and memos to write --
I must keep my brain clear, and priorities right.
The day is over, she checks with Dan when to meet.
Coming home together is still a treat.
Dan cooks supper, Marge brings me mine.
When hubby cooks, wife's face does shine.

Marjorie loads the dishwasher and makes the kitchen neat,
Then sinks into the lazy-boy chair to rest her tired feet.
A call comes down from the room above:
'Oh Marjorie, come here. I need you, my love.'
You can't guess what I've done today.
Oh yes. Another poem to be typed is underway.
But you type well; it turns out so neat.
And to have it computer stored is an important feat.
There's shopping, laundry, doctor's appointment at three;
Then get groceries, supper to prepare -- poor me, poor me!
'It's better to wear out than to rust out' I've heard it said.
'Yes, well I'm tired and I'm going to bed.'
Good night.

A Resume of Marjorie's History

There are many things I like about Marjorie:
If I'm sick or well, her door is always open to me.
She was the last of the girls to leave our home,
Then it felt so empty and I felt so alone.

I like to think of the days gone by;
We went places together, how the time does fly!
Though my youngest daughter, she is my faithful pal.
I feel so honoured to have such a gal.

We went places and enjoyed the Lord,
And felt His blessing on us was poured.
She finished high school and won a hundred dollars,
And twelve trophies for being the best of the scholars.

Then a sad, sad day came along.
To Ryerson in Toronto she was bound.
I'd sell things and save, so I could go and see
All of my girls in Toronto - I missed them greatly.

A sad thing happened that broke my heart.
She went to the States, married, but her way was dark.
Problems so big, she had no way,
But Aunt Flossie went to see her one day.

By that time, she had a baby whom she called Rochelle.
The situation for the little one was too sad to tell.
Aunt Flossie said, "You don't have to put up with this, dear."
"Go back to Toronto, there'll be a way for you. Don't fear."

Flossie wrote letters telling of the sad situation
And suggested we do something to change her destination.
For this cause we did earnestly pray
And Dad sent a ticket for just one way.

I had an apartment which I was so happy to share,
With Marjorie and Rochelle; a beautiful answer to prayer.
Marge got a job through my friend's friend
With the TD Bank, that has had no end.

Step by step, she is now in management
And likes her work, in a relaxed environment.
These days together were happy for sure.
I enjoyed babysitting Shell, what needed I more?

It wasn't long until Marjorie had a car.
With it we travelled near and far.
It wasn't good -- always letting us down.
She went into a garage, and a new Subaru found.

It was paid for by what we had, and could borrow.
That bettered the garage visits of sorrow.
In four months, all of our debts were paid.
God blessed the money that Marjorie made.

We were happy together, everything worked out.
We both liked flying and travelling about.
Rochelle was funny in the things she'd say
And provided pleasure for travellers along the way.

Three moves we had before we came to this place.
We are still here. Thank God for His grace.
Marjorie got anxious for a husband to find.
No one seemed to come to her line.

Ten years later, at work, a man named Dan
Decided he'd found a girl. He'd like to hold her hand.
He loved her laugh and her winsome smile,
And when she sneezed, it was her style.

A budding romance did begin;
A year, a wedding, then Dan moved in.
Our family now numbered four.
Three generations of women, Dan endured.

I felt led to return to the Northland
And was warmly received by old-time friends.
Not long after that, Rochelle received Salvation.
Now in her life is a great transformation.

Miracles took place; she is now in Bible College.
Her soul is being saturated with anointed knowledge.
She is so happy, contented and blessed,
In love with Jesus, and manifesting His righteousness.

It brought such a blessing into this home.
Both Mum and Dad are happy for what God has done.
There is such a closeness and love manifest.
It's just the beginning, how God's going to bless.

I have a word of appreciation in my heart.
In this beloved family, I feel I have a part.
I love the open door and the welcome mat,
The loving help I receive, and even the cat.

Rochelle's Transformation

Prayer has ascended for those at "126".
Against Satan's strategy of evil tricks.
Rochelle was his special target, he set for his goal.
He filled her with sin and sadness; thought he had control.

Something happened. A wonderful change took place:
Rochelle found a loving Saviour, partook of His saving grace.
She is so happy now. Restoration has begun.
Instead of worldly lyrics, worship and praise is sung.

The thrill of her life is meetings, she's always eager to go,
Where the presence and anointing of Jesus sweetly flow.
Fellowship with man is God's great treasure.
His heavenly riches, given without measure,

Shall be received by those who are hungry and believe.
They treasure the Spirit, whom they try not to grieve.
In the beginning, Adam enjoyed Godly communion;
But his disobedience severed that union.

Eternal blessings he sold to wicked Satan,
Who plunged all humanity into his condemnation.
All Satan's dominion, Jesus overcame.
The sin problem was cancelled in Jesus' name.

But He made us with a will to decide,
Whom we'd serve, and with whom we'd abide.
It takes a quality decision -- an encounter with God,
To snap Satan's chains, and stand on the Word.

All our sins He bore, His life He has given
To prepare us for the next world from Heaven.
No way our natural life in that world can abide --
All that pertains to that life, in the natural has died:

A dog cannot produce kittens,
Neither can a pig nourish chickens.
A child can't live in water, or a fish play in the sand
All must abide in life's realm according to God's plan.

Thus a heavenly world needs a heavenly life,
Which Jesus alone can give.
Under His blessing and anointing
He empowers us His life to live.
God loves turning curses into blessing --
Angels are rejoicing over Rochelle's decision.

My Imagination Takes a Trip

I am going to take a trip in my imagination
And pay a visit to the Jim and Gladys' Plantation.
December 29th is when I think I'll go.
I won't be there, but what goes on, I think I know:
I come into the kitchen. Something smells so good.
I look around and see lots of food.
There is a cake on Gladys' fancy plate
Elaborately decorated. Its sure in fine shape.
The sink is filled with dishes, but "Let it be",
Says Mother, as she buzzes around like a honey bee.
I go into the dining room. The table is laid.
Gladys' good silver and dishes are nicely displayed.

A knock -- Laura runs. "I'll go see.
Its Auntie Ella! Do you have a present for me?"
'Well we could look in this bag and see what we can find.
I don't think I'd miss a pretty little niece like mine.'
"Another car has just pulled in", says Daddy Jim.
"Its Rhoda, Bob, Sharon and Brien! Come on in."
"Now, since all of our guests came,
Lets shut Grandma's tape off. We'll listen to her again."
OK. But don't stay away too long.
I'm going to play and sing for you, a nice song.
Before I do, there's a funny story I'd like to tell.
Its about your mum when she was a tiny gal:

It was Christmas time, and our concert was under way.
Children in costumes and crowns -- a beautiful display.
At attention they all did stand.
A homemade musical instrument was held in their hand.
Gladys looked cute as by the piano she stood.
She giggled and kept time and was playing very good.
Her crown slipped, bobbing up and down on her nose.
She didn't stop playing. Folk laughed, it tickled them so.
Helen fixed the crown, piano played left handed -- so sweet.
The music didn't stop, neither lost they a beat.
The recital was over. They laughed and they clapped.
They had never seen an instrumental just like that.

18

Of all the features on that Christmas program,
Nothing topped that ingenious homemade band.
The funniest thing of it all,
Was when Gladys' crown on her nose did fall.
Helen replaced it so harmoniously,
It looked like it belonged and was supposed to be.
I want to sing a couple Chinese songs if I can.
Our girls sang them at our D.V.B.S. program...
Now I'm going to play and sing for you,
And don't you laugh -- you sing too!
"Yes, Jesus loves me. Yes, Jesus loves me."
And "Jesus loves the little children."

What happens now, I really don't know.
I expect supper is over and the guests have to go,
But they did the dishes, put everything back right,
So dear, tired Gladys doesn't have to work half the night.
Now the rest of the tape is special, don't you see,
For two little girls who are special to me.
One is Laura, one is Angela. Each has a pretty name.
Lets ask Ben, Elizabeth, and Morgan to join our game:
Likely Ben is still hopping around.
His leg is in a cast so he's bobbing up and down.
He thinks to himself, 'Its not bad being laid up this way.
I don't do any work -- I'm just enjoying a holiday!'

'I don't bring in wood or have to carry water.
Chores are left for busy mum and Elizabeth, her daughter.'
Elizabeth gives him a look of disgust:
"As soon as that cast is off -- work you must!"
There are no chickens or ducks or bunnies in the pen.
There are lots of kittens and Morgan looks after them.
Maybe she's sitting in the big kitchen chair
No homework to do or lessons to prepare.
I was interested to hear how dear Ben got home
From away in the pasture, with a broken bone.
Elizabeth called mum who got the horse ready to go
To get Ben who was laying in the snow.
Now Ben is hefty, the mare is tall. Its a problem we know

19

They got her in a valley, Mother heaved with all her might,
Ben got his good leg over, so they made it alright.
She walked nicely through the deep snow.
Elizabeth led her where they wanted to go.
Ben had a problem getting down.
The mare got impatient and whirled around.
Ben went flying down to the ground and let out a yell.
He hoped she knew that she hurt him when he fell.
They got him to the hospital. They put him in a cast;
Because he's a strong, healthy boy, they expect it'll heal fast.
His bones are strong and in good condition,
So we look for a speedy recovery with no complications.

Now Ben, please don't take that ski-doo back there again.
Its too much hassle, too much fuss, and too much pain.
Regardless of the problem, your mum found a way out.
When you all pulled together, it helped without a doubt.
Laura, I think by now you go to school all day,
And you're finding out this learning business isn't all play.
Can you write words? I'd like to get a letter from you;
See the pretty pictures you draw and the nice things you do.
Before long, Angela will be waiting for the bus. What fun!
Mother's baby daughter's school days so quickly have come.
Time flies by, children grow so fast;
We wonder why baby days don't a little longer last.

School days too, so quickly are gone,
We find ourselves sitting at home alone.
We wonder, "Have I done all I could do
To impress upon my dear children life's value?"
"Did I seek to build character that is honest and kind;
Stick to their word; be dependable. Keep a clear mind;
To set themselves for the right and hate the wrong;
Serve the Lord with all of their heart; sing a song."
"Pride, selfishness, anger, wrath, greed and unforgiving,
Adultery, fornication, unbelief, drunkenness and evil talking;
None of these can enter Heaven -- all go to a terrible Hell.
Make the right choice, so with your soul it is well."

My First Trip to Jerusalem

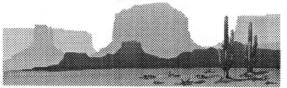

I cannot find words to express how I feel
Regarding the revelations on this trip, and the Spirit's seal.
Dear Lord, many things have left a deep impression;
Please bring them forth with Your blessing.

My heart is full of appreciation for dear Uncle Jim:
Many times he came to my rescue; so please bless him.
Beloved Sister Gwen and the other sisters too,
Were so loving and helpful as they manifested You.

Thank You for giving us two outstanding men
Who unsparingly gave themselves to us again and again.
Joseph and Moses, whom You know by name,
Joseph, an excellent driver and Moses, our trips did explain.

Those narrow mountain roads with hair-pin curves,
Meeting large vehicles, was enough to shatter his nerves.
Once I looked down and caught my breath;
But our expert driver saved us from death.

Moses went 30 miles extra to show us an impressive sight;
I thought of our driver and wondered if it was right.
Joseph was willing, even at the end of a hard day;
Live not for yourself but others, he did daily display.

Moses so aptly the Word did entwine;
Old Testament characters are beloved friends of mine.
It thrilled me to see the tombs where they were laid
After an eternal history, they had made.

My spirit in me was awed as we went from place to place;
And was enlarged by God's wisdom and unfathomable grace.
O Lord, I want to thank You for the strength You gave me
To do what many thought was beyond my ability.

At the Feast of Tabernacles, Your glory came down;
I thought how dearly You love Your own.
Now Jerusalem and the Hebrews mean much more to me,
A special people in a special place, formed for Your glory.

Shall I tread that soil again? I do not know.
Thank You Lord, for making it possible for me to go;
May the imprint of this blessing go deep in my soul;
Make me more intimate with You, 100% under Your control.

Galilee

Five provinces surround this harp-shaped sea.
Most of Jesus' ministry was on the shores of Galilee.
Much of the biblical records here takes place.
Jesus manifests His Father's power, glory, and grace.

Here by the beautiful sea of Galilee
Jesus began His God given ministry.
His first miracle was turning water to wine.
Such a thing surely blew their mind. 1

Jesus began revealing to people, His loving Father;
The fulfilment of many prophesies, that very hour.
In the Nazareth synagogue, He took the Book and read:
Today is fulfilled what Isaiah has said. 2

They marvelled as His gracious words did flow
With power and authority, God's love He did bestow.
He healed all who to Him came;
Always giving the glory to His Father's name.

22

He healed the woman with the issue of blood.
She said: "If I can but touch His garment, I can be healed."
Daughter, thy faith hath made thee whole. 3
He healed her body and gave her peace in her soul.

Jarius' twelve year old daughter almost died.
To Jesus, he beseechingly cried.
Someone came and said:
"Trouble not the Master. She is already dead."

Jesus said: "Fear not. Only believe,
And your answer you shall receive."
He came to his house and said: "Maid arise".
And the mocking crowd got a surprise. 4

Thousands came to hear His words of comfort and joy,
And He fed them all with the lunch of a little boy.
There were twelve baskets full left that day. 5
Each of the twelve had one to enjoy along the way.

He healed Peter's mother-in-law and then
She arose and ministered unto them.. 6
All who had diverse diseases,
That evening they brought them to Jesus. 7

Jesus in loving compassion, healed every one.
His fame throughout the country run. 8
In Geneseret, many pressed upon Him to hear the gospel,
So He sat in Peter's boat the glorious gospel to tell.

Peter, push out. Let down your net for a draught.
Lord, we fished all night, and not one we caught.
Peter obeyed, and the net got so full, it was ready to break.
His friends quickly came, the overflow to take. 9

---

1. John 2: 6-11   2. Luke 4:16-32
3. Luke 8:44-48   4. Luke 8:49-55
5. Luke 14:14-21   6. Luke 4:38
7. Luke 4:40   8. Mark 4:1
9 Luke 5:56

At Capernaum, Jesus sent Peter to catch a fish in the sea.
In its mouth would be a coin for their tax money. [1]
Jesus stopped a funeral at the gate of Nain,
And gave a weeping widow, her son, alive again. [2]

There was a special mountain where Jesus loved to go.
There He taught the beatitudes, He wants us all to know.
Rochelle and I walked where Jesus walked [3]
And visited the places where He taught.

We had a beautiful trip across the sea.
Anointed singing and praising, we felt His glory.
With this anointed group, I loved to be.
It made me think of the joy for eternity.

They took us through a museum, Peter's boat to see.
It was an awesome sight and greatly impressed me;
How it was found, rescued, preserved, was a story of grace.
All the solutions involved, just fell into place.

God made the waters go lower than every they had been.
The shape of the boat buried in sand, by two men was seen.
Men and women removed the sand with their hands
Most carefully, so as not to harm the frail boat's identity.

All things were ready, but to move it, they needed a way.
Back came the water, and floated it to safety.
Top scientists came and made a pickle-like solution,
Saturated the wood, to stabilize it from further deterioration.

There was a small place for a pillow, Peter had made,
And on that pillow, Jesus' head He laid. [4]
All these details seemed to say
God preserved this boat in a remarkable way.

---

[1]. Matthew 17:27   [2]. Luke 7:11-14
[3]. Matthew 5:1-12   [4]. Mark 4:38
[5]. Revelation 10:2,6

Noah's ark on Mount Ararat and Peter's boat in the sea,
In our day, has a message of warning, it seems to me.
Many other discoveries prove the accuracy of God's word.
These are acts of mercy of our gracious Lord.

Many sceptical people, the truth cannot receive.
These infallible proofs should help them to believe.
What God has declared, is coming to pass with no mistake.
It's high time now, for us to hear and be awake.

An angel shall stand, one foot on land and one on the sea,
And loudly proclaim, time no longer shall be. 5
As horrifying as the great tribulation shall be,
It cannot equal Hell for eternity.

If we live for the flesh, we'll reap corruption.
If we live for God, we'll reap life everlasting.
God's end time program is now underway.
Prophesies about Israel, show the closeness of that day.

We marvelled at the accuracy and beauty of Jerusalem.
But it cannot compare to the new one, soon to come.
There are many things I've not been able to touch,
Of our trip to Israel, which we enjoyed very much.

A Different Brand of Charity

At a Lakehead Senior Home, I went to see
A very dear friend with whom I love to be.
It was a cold night, and a bad storm.
Her apartment was cheerful, homey, and warm.

She called: "Mabel, come quickly and you will see
A different brand of love and charity."
I saw an old man, moving slowly, but well clad.
Under his arm, a container of grain, he had.

He put it in a certain place,
Then returned with a smile on his face.
"Now be still, and watch, and you will see --
Something will come to eat, presently."

Out jumped a beautiful buck and his little doe.
They seemed to know right where to go.
I was glad it was near the window, so I could see
This unique scene, I enjoyed immensely.

They finished the grain, then jumped out of sight.
At least they would not be hungry that night.
God bless that man who had gotten to know
That beautiful buck and his little doe.

An Impressive Bus Ride

I took a trip to western Canada by bus
Via the prairie route in late August.
Good fields of grain I was happy to see
As I thought of their sad state formerly.

The loss sustained by locusts and drought
Caused hard working farmers to be wiped out
Farther west more evidence of drought I see
Which inevitably will cause great misery.

Brown parched pastures did not look good;
My heart ached as animals sought for food.
Farmers were resourceful, as I could see
That irrigation was working effectively.

I had an awesome dream filled with dread:
Grain flattened as snow over it spread.
I felt sick and hoped it was just a dream.
Later on TV I saw what I had already seen.

If grain is slow to mature,
The frost, it shall not endure.
If grain is too light it will be lost --
A heartache to farmers, at a great cost.

God's judgement on sin is seen far and wide
All man's wisdom shall not stem the tide.
God's wrath poured out is beyond control,
Caused by the evil of our sin cursed soul.

Like grain, we also must be hard and mature
Or church cleansing we shall not endure.
The temple twice cleansed in His ministry.
So the church is sin purged, and set free.

A Trip to the North-Land by Train

The train is moving slowly heading for the North-lands.
There are people on the platform waving their hands.
Once again I say good-bye with a lonesome pain;
This great Toronto -- I'm leaving you again.

It's gaining speed as it winds its way through the Don Valley.
I'm amazed how it finds such thick forest all of the way.
Only a few houses and buildings can be seen,
But I admire those trees in their various green.

They differ in size and shape and colour,
But they make a wall as they huddle together.
They put down their roots and grow so tall --
On each side of the train is a green wall.

They are rooted in the same earth, and live the same way,
As they manifest the great Creator's beauty.
When the fierce wind blows, they bend but don't break,
Because they stand together in their place unique.

This is the message to my heart, it spake:
We're different, yet placed by Him, our ground to stake.
This is what we need to do in our church today:
Stand together and support each other in God's way.

They are not the same, but they stand as one
And support each other against the storms that come.
God through nature teaches us His will;
If we listen, His purpose in us He'll fulfil.

White fluffy clouds beautify the sky.
They are changing shape. Look at that -- like a bobcat.
There is a hole for its eye and the blue shines through.
The train rounds a bend and I lose my view.

I like to see the iron horse go down the trail
Then I look in the other direction and see its tail.
Riding this shaky train, for me is a feat.
I find myself draping over someone else's seat.

Children walk down the isle as if the train was still.
What is wrong with me? I guess I am over the hill.
That's why I like Rochelle to travel with me --
She is such a help and blessing. I'm sure you'll agree.

There is Lake Simcoe. Rhoda lives across that water.
I pray for her family and her, my first born daughter.
That iron horse is speeding down the woods again.
I'm cloud gazing, to see what else is plain.

There is a lion and he is ready to spring;
And the train turns and did the same thing.
There is a bear. It's lying down but raised it's head.
That too was gone as the train onward sped.

I'm going to close my eyes and rest a bit
But my imagination just won't quit.
The jolts and bumps make me think
Of a Pacific boat ride -- some thought we'd sink.

There is North Bay. It must be five or thereabouts.
In almost three hours I'll leave this rocky boat.
We are in Tamagami reserve. It seems more rough.
When I reach New Liskeard, I think I will have had enough.

Days are getting longer. There is a difference in the trees.
Hard wood in the south are now soft wood predominately.
In the fall, hard wood have a beautifully coloured array.
Soft wood has only different shades of yellow to display.

Could that be the Ottawa river we are winding around?
Many streams and lakes in this beautiful reserve are found.
Tamagami is a pretty place. Some men are casting nets
Which brings back northern memories I just cannot forget.

A more rocky area and there is Cobalt that bald-headed hill -
Silver used to be mined here. Now those machines are still.
Likely all those miners are gone who dug that ore.
Cobalt expresses a land that is poor.

I'm about ready bid this train good-bye.
I'm still impressed by the beautiful sky.
Soon those clouds will roll back like a scroll --
Suddenly Jesus will come to rapture my soul.

I'll have my last train-ride and say good-bye the last time.
I'll be with my Lover forever and His glory shall be mine.
Please give me a clean wine-skin, dear Lord I pray;
Just to contain You and do my part in Your ministry today.

Norman is waiting for me. He looks sick and in pain.
He walks with a limp and is using his cane again.
He tells me he was doing very, very well,
Until a dog dashed in front of him and he fell.

Grandma's imagination can surely run wild.
She's old now and sometimes acts like a child;
But we love her and we tell her so,
And we scratch our head -- where next will she go?

Lost in the Bush

We walked twelve miles to go to Sunday School;
It was winter and the weather was cool.
We enjoyed our friends when together we met --
The way they prayed, I'll never forget.

Molly invited us home -- what a treat;
She didn't have much but she was so sweet.
She was to me a very dear sister;
In the winter time, I surely missed her.

The next morning I heard my brother say
He was going home a shorter way.
It would save seven miles, but wouldn't you know --
There was a mile where you had to wade snow!

The fellowship was so sweet, I decided to stay
For a few more days and then go home the same way
I left around two while the sun shone bright;
Molly prayed that I would make it home alright.

On our window from Alabon's crest, the sun did shine;
The homeward trail seemed to be a straight line.
From the top of the hill, I could see my front door --
Three miles to go but the time was now four.

I skied down the slope and got a surprise;
A very good road then met my eyes.
I hurried along as fast as I could go,
Glad indeed not to have to wade snow.

I shortly became troubled and wondered what to do;
It didn't deem that the road went through.
Suddenly then a sad thing I found,
In the green bush, the road turned around.

It looks like the end, "Lord, now what do I do?"
'Just turn to the right and you will get through.'
"Thank you Dear Lord, that sounds so sweet,
Just lead me on and guide my feet."

No trail at all through the brush and the trees,
It was difficult going on those homemade skis.
They would get caught and down I would go --
And had to dig myself out of a pile of loose snow.

The daylight was fading, it would soon be dark;
I had a scary feeling around my heart.
"Oh Lord, now where am I, I do not know --"
And then I heard a rooster crow!

I pressed on and on -- It was now quite dark,
But my heart was cheered by a little dog's bark.
That was much closer, what a thrill to me --
Then through the trees a field I could see.

The moon had risen so full and so bright;
The mercury was sinking; it was a cold night.
I could see a friend's house on the river bank --
For that sight, my Lord I did sincerely thank.

The bush was snapping, the fog was hanging;
I crossed a large field, I felt my strength waning.
I made it through to my friend's back door
And almost fell on her kitchen floor.

Such a visitor! What a surprise!
When I told my story, she opened her eyes.
"God was good to you without a doubt --
Its an amazing thing how you got out."

We had a good supper; I enjoyed the time;
I guess I left for home around nine.
"May I leave these skis outside your door? --
I'd rather walk home than ski anymore."

"Oh Mabel, It is such a cold night,
Are you sure you can make it home alright?"
"Oh, yes, the moon is bright and it's a good road;
I'm a good runner when I have no load."

I still had a mile and a half to go,
But I knew I could make it in twenty minutes or so.
I was so grateful for the nourishment I had,
For all I'd been through, I wasn't doing too bad.

I ran and ran until I could run no more
And was so glad when I reached our door.
Norman was shocked when I staggered in,
"On such a cold night, where have you been?"

"Well, I came down the hill and a good road I found,
But it went down to a swamp then turned around.
There wasn't a trail eastward that I could see,
But the Dear Lord had mercy upon me."

"I had a strong feeling to turn to the right,
And if I kept going, I'd come out alright.
I came to a field when the moon was so bright --
I got a thrill to see Myrtle's bright light."

"Myrtle gave me supper and thought it best
That I stay awhile and have a rest.
I felt much better for that I can say
And from their home I ran most of the way."

Norman took the same road but waded the snow
And came to the river up a mile or so.
We then agreed with the words of a poem:
"The longest way around is the safest way home".

The demons contended for my life that night.
They made me think the easy way was right.
I ought to have stopped right there to pray
And avoided such a hike at the close of the day.

"All the way my Saviour leads me,
What have I to ask besides?
Can I doubt His tender mercy,
Who through life has been by Guide?"

Charged By a Bull

Mother called, "Mabel go get the cows, its milking time",
It was early but nice in the warm bright sunshine.
Our little dog Collie was very smart --
When he heard the bell, he was off like a dart.

I just waited on top our gravel pit hill;
Sure enough, down the trail came the cows with a will.
It saved me getting wet with the morning dew,
There were a lot of bushes I'd have to go through.

I thought, "If I run with all of my might,
Put my hands on the top bar -- I'd go over alright."
I did it, which to me was a great surprise;
But I couldn't believe what then met my eyes:

The bull we had raised was charging me;
For some reason, he was mad as could be.
Then down on one knee, hooking stones in the air,
His roars and his bellows sure gave me a scare!

I ran to the house all out of breath
And told them how I had just escaped death --
I ran real fast, flipped over the fence,
So wasn't there to receive the consequence.

I thought I'd do it again, but wouldn't you know --
Over the bars my feet would not go.
I knew it right there and then,
My angel had spared my life again.

One time before I was mowing hay,
The team decided to run away.
They were heading straight for a deep ditch --
I knew if they hit it, I'd sure get pitched.

I let down the blade, gave the gear a kick --
The sudden jolt stopped the horses real quick.
Mollie's bit had somehow come out,
And she was going to the barn the shortest route.

The jolt nearly knocked them off their feet,
I quickly jumped from the mower seat.
I grabbed her head replaced the bit,
Patted her nose and told her, "We'd quit."

I unhooked, then took them to the barn,
Glad indeed there was no harm.
It's a wonder to me the mower didn't break --
But again, the Lord did undertake.

As I look back many times I can see,
The dear Lord had mercy upon me.
I got saved when I was twelve -- what a night!
My sins all were gone and I felt so light.

To my pals I said, something good happened to me,
And now I am happy as happy can be.
They said, "Oh we heard.", but turned away,
And with me then they would not play.

I didn't mind. I was so happy inside,
And glad the Lord I had not denied.
It was easy to testify and pray;
I wanted to be a missionary someday.

I am glad I'm a Christian and learned to pray,
I know the Lord hears everything I say.
There have been times I knew not what to do,
But God in His mercy made a way through.

"He shall give his angels charge over thee." Psalms 91:11

Blow Off Where it Pays Off

Its OK to blow off to Jesus. He will answer you;
But don't try it on people; it just won't do.
A sister said something not nice about me.
I was hurt and as cross as I could be.

'Lord, I walked five miles on a cold winter day
To stay with her when her husband was away.'
She didn't appreciate the five mile walk I had.
To say such a thing made me feel very sad.

"Do you appreciate what I have done for you?"
And a vision passed before my view:
A lacerated Body, His strength at a loss,
He staggered and fell beneath a heavy cross.

"It was by My stripes you were healed."
My own ungrateful heart was revealed.
'Oh no, Lord, I don't appreciate what You've done', I cried,
'Please forgive me!' ...Then He sweetly replied:

"Whatever you do, do it heartily for Me, not for man.
They will forget you, but I never can."
I then was delighted with what happened that day;
For it made me appreciate Jesus in a real way.

A Good Teacher

Don't be too sure, of what you're so sure about.
You could be wrong when the truth comes out.
This is a valuable lesson, we all must take:
Dead sure we're right, then, Oh no, its a mistake.

To receive mercy, show mercy. Truth shall be revealed.
Innocence acquitted, and the guilty sealed.
Things do turn up -- a surprise from where.
So in everything give thanks, and you'll win in prayer.

Irene had my change purse, but put it back in my hand.
Where it went from there, I couldn't understand.
I looked and looked -- where could it be?
Lord, I'm looking no more, until You show me.

Two weeks later, Irene called to say:
I'll come and help you find it today.
No, I've quit looking until Jesus tells me where.
As I played the piano, He said: It's down in that chair.

I reached my hand down, clear out of sight.
There was my purse. It was quite alright.
Lord, nothing misses Your all seeing eye.
It was just another lesson, on You to rely.

Lord Jesus, engage my heart today
With a zeal that will not pass away,
And purge me with Your holy fire,
Anointed to do Your heart's desire --
So every effort, to You shall bring
Rapturous praise to my Lord and King.

To Forget -- A Blessing!

I knew what I wanted two seconds ago!
It's gone now, and why, I do not know.
Oh Lord, help, and tell me why I'm here.
Back came the answer, and very clear.

His all seeing eye is ever upon me,
And shows His love so beautifully.
Forgetfulness is not my cup of tea.
When Jesus helps, it makes me happy.

Yesterday's experience I'd like to share,
For in a good way, I felt His loving care.
I returned a water unit. It wasn't practical.
I forgot that I got a cartridge to be available.

But where did I put it, I'd like to know.
From my mind, that cartridge did fully go.
I was about to ask Irene to pray with me.
A whisper in my heart said, 'Just let it be.'

I was happy and not even thinking about it,
When I saw a little vision in the Spirit:
My hand reaching up to put it out of the way.
I opened a top door. It was there plain as day.

I do not like limitations, I truthfully say,
But depending on Jesus is a profitable way.
He loves us and wants the elderly to know,
His grace is sufficient, if His way we go.

It's the little things in life
That determine the big things.   Matthew 23:21

I have held many things in my hands and lost them all.
The things I put in God's hands, I always possess.
                                        II Timothy 1:12

Another Farewell

There had been several farewells at the church in Hearst,
But at this one, my heart felt like it would burst.
It seemed like the backbone of the little church had gone;
It was in poor shape when Bruce and Kaye Swintz had come.

They were full of love, courage and zeal.
A quickening Spirit we began to feel.
To support the work was a struggling feat.
The Swintz had a hard time to make ends meet.

For their few years of ministry, I was very glad.
Now they were leaving, I was very sad.
The party was over. It was time to go home.
Most of the guests from the country had come.

It was our responsibility to see it through.
The means of conveyance were our cars, just two.
It was thundering, lightning, and starting to rain --
To take a big load in our old car was a strain.

I didn't want to do it, but there was no way out.
Connie came with me; she was such a good scout.
The road was rough by the railroad track;
Apart from lightning, the night was black.

The lights were so poor I could hardly see,
And the rain came down abundantly.
The windshield wipers then laid still --
Visibility now was reduced to nil.

39

A sweet Presence, we both did feel:
I felt a hand placed on the wheel.
We made the curves on that lonely dark road,
In safety turned around, and delivered our load.

The highway was under construction and hard to get past.
Again my Angel helped me, and we got safe home at last.
I laid my sleeping children on the bed,
Took down the receiver, Bruce's troubled voice said:

'Mabel, did you make it home alright?
I've been phoning and phoning -- its such a bad night.'
"Yes, praise the Lord, I made it through,
But a trip like that, I don't care to do."

The Lord is so gracious, nothing is too hard for Him.
He kept the car under control with the lights so dim.
That trip reminds me of life's pathway here below:
Jesus our Saviour knows where and how to go.

Dear Marjorie has asked me to write this poem
In praise to Father, Who brought us safe home.
Through the storms of life, from paths of sin,
My girls and their families, please bring them in.

Father in Heaven, I know You hear my prayer,
That my loved ones end not up in eternal despair.
Fill with Your righteousness, peace, joy, and love.
Let their vision be captured, with life from above.

These are the children which God has graciously given me:

"I will contend with him that contendeth with thee.
And I will save thy children."   Isaiah 49:25
"I set my face like a flint,
And I know I shall not be ashamed."   Isaiah 50:7
"And all thy children shall be taught of the Lord:
And great shall be the peace of thy children." Isaiah 54:13
"And all things, whatsoever ye shall ask in prayer,
Believing, ye shall receive."   Matthew 21:22

The Destroyer
and The Restorer
of Families

I worked hard, but I had a song,
I wasn't expecting anything to go wrong.
I thought that I was special, my husband did too;
We didn't think anything very wrong we would do.

I wanted a model family and everything right,
Lots of love and fun and continual delight.
We got so involved in a good living to make,
Something very important we did forsake.

There was no time to read the Bible and pray,
We did our own thing the whole live long day.
Our life hasn't worked out the way I had planned;
Our home life is not all that grand.

I love my children with a Mother's heart.
They have been my sunshine and of my life a great part;
But selfishness, anger and greed, raid our home;
We get hurt, upset and angry -- what a sad outcome.

What happened to the happiness I thought I had found?
Why did my air plane come to the ground?
Is there a word for a troubled soul?
How do I get these things under control?

My child, your home is not founded on My Word and prayer;
So the devil came in and caused trouble and despair --
To destroy and wreck families he has carefully planned;
So many souls will be eternally damned.   John 10:10

Lord, I really don't know You; nor You're Word understand.
I thought with my wisdom, my life I could command.
I could see others were wrong and myself always right;
When my ego was challenged, I was ready to fight.

With my pride, self-sufficiency, and vain mind,
A way to change my life style, I cannot find.
But my limitations does not limit You;
You died to save me, and I know Your Word is true.

Please forgive me and make me all over again;
On the citadel of my soul, come in and reign.
Grant Your love to come in, and our fleshly traits go;
So we will be a testimony to everyone we know.

I need Your faith, Spirit and courage, to obey,
And a spiritual ear to hear what You say.
To help my family, which I want you to save,
That they end not up in an ungodly grave.

"Take time, take time to read My Word;   Proverbs 1:23
The Spirit shall reveal your restoration in the Lord.
You must be willing to seek Me with all of your heart,
And let me sanctify you and set you apart."   Hebrews 9:10

I sanctified Myself in the garden for you;
I knew full well what I would have to go through.
I knew the awful price of the blood that had to be paid.
Thy will not Mine. Drops of blood fell as I prayed

It was the hardest battle ere fought, in the garden for you.
Thus I am able to be your sanctifier too.
Only if you are willing to repent, be cleansed and set apart,
Then sanctified and purified, to be My counterpart.

If you could only see the joy and the glory that awaits
The faithful, who shall enter the pearly gates,
You would consider no price too high to pay --
The most glorious manifestation is for My saints today.

It is the greatest privilege granted to man,
And don't think you can't make it -- with Me you can.
The great coming sorrow exceeding all that has gone before,
Will be too devastating for you to endure.

Eph. 1:6; Zeph. 1:14-18; Isa. 10:3; Rev. 19:9, 20:12, 21:8

God Will See You Through

I am confident God will see you through.
I am confident He'll work all things out for you.
Appreciate His sweet love and the power of His call.
The special plan, He ordained for you before the fall.

He has blessed you with His presence and Spirit.
The gifts He has given are able to manifest it.
All worldly systems are against God.
All our carnal nature joins their hoard.

God made you a house of clay
To be to His name praise, honour, and glory.
The devil likes to mess up our circumstance
But Jesus is there to bless with His abundance.

Don't let anything distress or cause you to doubt.
The Holy Spirit in you knows how to work it out.
No matter how big the devil may seem.
He's no match for Jesus, Who stands between.

Did you know Jesus has a special plan for you?
Your talents, and personality is designed for His groove.
You can't figure it out. You have no way.
Just simply rely on His word. Praise and pray.

A special strategy He has for you.
Its a hundred percent foolproof and scripturally true.
It starts with genuine repentance and turning from sin;
A dedicated decision to live wholeheartedly for Him.

To be a good stewardess of what He's intrusted to you,
According to His will and purpose, long to be true.
Make room for the precious Holy Spirit to operate
In love, joy, peace and power, which He will demonstrate.

Get ready for an explosion of the Spirit within
That will blow out the carnality of selfishness and sin.
Such joy and rejoicing shall flood over your soul.
There's such peace and satisfaction when He is in control.

There is a style to which we must carefully look.
It is faithfulness and it begins in our pocket book.
This is a powerful hinge that opens a door of blessing.
God's precious promises are wrapped up in cheerful giving.

The next key in the strategy God has for us,
Is to be a good fisherman, God's main purpose.
We go where hungry fish are, and give them to eat
Of a big Jesus, Who can all their troubles meet.

You teach them to pray a repentant prayer.
Pull them into your boat, a church, God's riches to share.
They are now a part of the Body of our Lord.
You nourish them by feeding them the living Word.

The Holy Spirit in you has the key.
He knows the hungry fish awaiting your ministry.
There's such a thrill when obedient to His leading,
And such a satisfaction when hungry fish you are feeding.

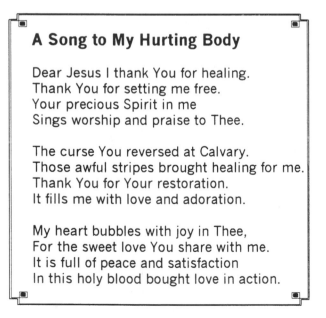

A Song to My Hurting Body

Dear Jesus I thank You for healing.
Thank You for setting me free.
Your precious Spirit in me
Sings worship and praise to Thee.

The curse You reversed at Calvary.
Those awful stripes brought healing for me.
Thank You for Your restoration.
It fills me with love and adoration.

My heart bubbles with joy in Thee,
For the sweet love You share with me.
It is full of peace and satisfaction
In this holy blood bought love in action.

Line Up With the Pattern

Fully satisfy my love in You.
Make it living, burning, pure, and true,
That Father's love be shed abroad in my mind.
What I think, say, and do be brought in line.

Now I want to browse through Your Word and see
How it can make me like Thee.
I think I'll start with Isaiah forty-three
And see how You value humanity.

I want to personalize Your Word in prayer
So it can have the transforming effect, it does declare.
I want to feel the loving, longing of Your heart
To prepare me for Your Counterpart.

"I'm your Lord. I paid the ransom for thee. 1
You are precious in My sight. You were made for Me. 2
You are created in My glory to go in the way I have made.
I'm always with you, so don't be afraid."

"You are My chosen witness, I want you to see 3
The almighty God, your Saviour abideth in thee.
I want you to know and understand
What it means to be a chosen shaft in My hand."

"I have carefully formed you so you could be
A drink to My people for My glory. 4
I've blotted out your transgressions and sin.
I am your Justifier Who abides within." 5

"My law is perfect. It makes the simple wise. 6
It rejoices the heart, and enlightens the eyes.
Let your meditations on Me be sweet.
I am your Redeemer, none can defeat." 7

---

1. Isaiah 43:3   2. Isaiah 43:21
3. Isaiah 43:10,11   4. Isaiah 43:20,21
5. Isaiah 43:25,26   6. Psalms 19:7,8
7. Psalms 19:14

"According to My heart, My counsel I'll fulfill,
And anoint you to stand in the gap, doing My will. 1
In unity, shout the praises of your Lord. 2
My blessing will be upon you, declaring My Word." 3

There will be times my spirit is overwhelmed within; 4
By the word of Thy lips, I will be kept from sin. 5
"It is all to teach you to do My will 6
So just trust in Me and learn to be still." 7

"The Lord thy God hath opened thine ear.
Awaken each morning, My voice to hear. 8
Don't turn back and do not rebel. 9
Enjoy gladness and thanks giving. All is well." 10

"Don't spend money for that which is not bread.
Hearken diligently unto Me", the Lord hath said. 11
He sees and knows when giving is a sacrifice. 12
A great reward He'll give you if you pay the price.

Money is a tell-tale of our love for Him
As we deny ourselves, our love will not get dim.
He loved to serve, and He loved to give.
This is the pattern He wants us to live.

---

1. Psalms 20:5   2. Psalms 22:16   3. Psalms 133:1,3
4. Psalms 142:3   5. Psalms 17:4   6. Psalms 119:11
7. Isaiah 50:10   8. Isaiah 50:4   9. Isaiah 50:5
10. Isaiah 51:3   11. Isaiah 55:2   12. Isaiah 21:1-3

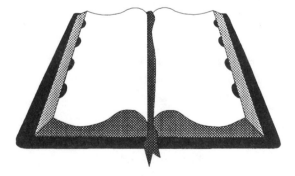

A Prayer for my Grandchildren

Lord Jesus, the only source of Peace today;
In this earthly chaos, do teach us to pray
And eagerly listen for Your direction,
To trust in Thee for our sure protection.

For my nine grandchildren, I earnestly plead:
In Your loving mercy, please meet their need.
A desire for Thee, put deep in each soul;
To be a willing vessel, under Your control.

Open wide their eyes and let them see
We're standing on the brink of eternity.
The prime thing in life is to be ready to die;
To be gloriously raptured with Jesus on High.

For those who know Him, all shall be well;
But those who don't, shall fall into Hell. [1]
You said my children would be taught of the Lord,
So grant Thine omnipotent Spirit on them be poured. [2]

Lord stretch forth Your arm that all may see,
Satan's destructiveness is no match for Thee.
Twenty-one woes shall make a speedy riddance of sin;
Then Your righteous Kingdom shall be ushered in.

---

1. Matthew 25: 12, 41, 46   2. Proverbs 1: 23

47

I Will Save thy Children

R. S. B. E. M. B. M. L. and A:
Are my grandchildren in order, for whom I pray:

Lord, grant faith, when their days are bright and sunny;
And grant faith, when the hours are dark and long;
Faith when things are going nicely;
And faith when everything seems to go wrong;
Faith when friendships are a blessing;
And faith even when loved ones prove untrue;
This very special blessing God has for each of you.

We all lack the fear of our loving Lord;
So we will pray this wisdom in us be poured.
Make us to abhor all evil and hate every bad word;
This is the gage that registers our fear of the Lord.
May Your Word fill us with an awesome respect;
That our relationship with Thee we will not neglect.

Rejecting the Truth leads to destroying the soul,
Which will inevitably bring it under Satan's control.
We can't thread a needle in the dark or untie a knot unseen;
Neither can we fight the enemy of our soul with our carnality

Lord Jesus come into our heart and forgive all of our sin;
You know what the enemy is up to. You are our help to win.
Thank You Lord for faith to bring them safely through.
If we don't give up on our children, neither will You.

"I, even I, am the Lord; and beside Me there is no Saviour."

Isaiah 43:11

A Part of Rick Joyner's Revelation

Two men in their earthly state, Rick was given to see.
"Which of these are more pleasing to Me?"
'The first.', Rick said without the least hesitation.
"No, the second." Now Rick was in frustration.
"I will tell you their stories, then you'll see
Why our judgments do not agree."

"The first was taught in a church that was alive;
Attended Bible College, had 100 measures of love.
He loved to pray for the sick, and teach zealously;
But with 25% he exulted his flesh, 75% exulted Me.
Outside he was good, but on the inside was pride
Which greatly alters rewards on the other side.

I judge not by outward appearances, but by the heart.
Submit to My judgments, to be My counterpart:
The other was deaf, dumb, abused, and alone.
He was institutionalized, then he was on his own.
Anger and wrath welled up in him like a high tide.
He wanted to kick a kitten, but just pushed it aside.

Angelo nearly starved but he quit stealing.
He collected bottles and did a little yard cleaning.
He had three measures of love, and he used it.
I was a stranger to him, and so was the Spirit.
He could not talk, but he learned to read.
I gave him a tract -- the Holy Spirit watered the seed.

He opened wide his heart for Me to come in.
I therefore doubled the love I had given him.
He bought a Bible and lived on its content
And manifested My love wherever he went.
Half of the little he had bought tracts for passers-by.
He led an alcoholic to Me who was about to die.

Angelo was so thrilled over that experience,
He would endure anything to bring deliverance.
He was grateful for a cardboard box on a cold night.
He loved Me so much, even in his poverty plight.
Angelo was a martyr every day he lived.
He ate just enough to live, so more he could give.

He was very faithful in all I had given,
Very few equalled his standard in living.
I called him home. All Heaven wanted him to come,
So I could give him the reward he nobly had won.
He didn't die for doctrine, he died for Me
And will reign a king, with Me for eternity.

He would have shared his love with you, but
You passed him by, and said he was a religious nut.
If you had taught him, you'd have received blessing,
Enjoyed a sweeter union with Me and more anointing.
In My law of love is delight, joy, peace, and rest.
If you manifest these wherever you go, you will bless.

'Lord, I'm really sorry. Please forgive me!' , I cried.
"You are forgiven", He quickly replied.
"Many unlearned and untrained are very sincere.
To Me, their hearts are very dear.
I brought you here so you could know and see
My righteous judgment and My love and mercy."

Angelo said, 'Remember my homeless friends.
They will be Jesus' lovers too, if you tell them.'
I couldn't speak, but my nod came from my heart.
'Lord, don't let this kingly decree ever depart.'
"The higher you walk in knowledge and authority,
The farther you will fall without love and humility."

The glory of God shall be revealed in such a way,
Every power on Earth shall witness His authority.
To know our God in such a special way, is available.
To be one in this army is the greatest honour possible.
Children, women, young and old in this manifestation
Will receive a reward beyond all our imagination.
50

Prophesy Fulfilled

Brother Copeland tells a story that will give you a thrill
About a man, because of his record, they were going to kill.
Kenneth preached the gospel to him, in his cell one day.
He told him God loved him, and taught him to pray.

He got wonderfully saved and filled with the Spirit.
Kenneth gave him a Bible. He read it and read it.
He was greatly transformed reading the Word with delight.
He was so full of joy, the death sentence caused no fright.

They put a needle into his arm vein.
Injecting poisons, that likely caused pain.
So in love with the Lord, Whom he had gotten to know;
This was a way to be with Him. He was willing to go.

Before the edict was transacted they let him tell
The story of his salvation, that rescued him from Hell:
I hold nothing in my heart against you. Do what you must do
There is just Jesus' love there, that is reaching out to you.

He preached such a message in simplicity and power;
Such reality staggered them, in that awful death hour.
Such victims, greatly struggle in horror, at what they face,
As their sad, sad life ends in remorseful disgrace.

They strapped him to the table, but got a big surprise --
Suddenly he fell in asleep, as he peacefully closed his eyes.
He slept so soundly, exceedingly loud he did snore,
And was absolutely unconscious, to what he was there for.

His death, by man had been planned
But an abundant entrance was planned in Glory Land.
All Heaven rejoiced, at the great victory won.
Such a masterpiece of Salvation, had just been done.

I think those executors, that snoring would never forget.
If they do not repent, for eternity they will hear it yet.
This story should help us God's Word to treasure,
And seek to obey Him, to the fullest measure.

Faith in God Defeated the Foe

I heard a testimony at the Christian Centre Sunday night
From a young Russian Brother who was in a sad plight.
The army sent him a forceful command:
You join the army, or in jail you will land!

'Father in heaven, what shall I do?'
"Go to Canada. I'll make a way for you."
My spirit gave a leap with a heavenly thrill --
Regardless of limitations, I'll do God's will.

I gathered up all I had and went to see
If there was a ticket available for me.
"Where are you going?", a young man asked.
'I'm going to Canada, as soon as I get a pass.'

"Man, you are in Russia, don't you know --
It will be four years before they let you go?"
This is what my Sovereign God told me to do.
I'm believing Him to make a way through.

I have a feeling I'm going to-day;
Let's go and see what they have to say.
"There are two seats available" he said with hesitation.
"Come back at noon for the confirmation."

Eight minutes after twelve, I was back at the wicket.
It took all I had, but I paid for my ticket.
I knew Father wasn't misinformed on my situation.
I had an awesome feeling as I waited in expectation.

I sat with my hands face upward on my bowed head.
'Father, thank You for my ticket, but there's no daily bread.'
Suddenly something was placed in my hands. I looked to see
Two thousand rubles had just been given to me!

A man was looking at me with tender eyes.
He smiled, enjoying my delighted surprise.
Was he a man or an angel? I did not know.
This gift was from Father. I knew I would go.

52

I praised my Lord as I sat on that plane
And my spirit rejoiced -- God does reign!
The battle is not over, was stirring in my soul --
Father, whatever happens, You are in control.

I felt apprehensive as the plane rolled in.
Soon the battle with immigration did begin.
The situation became very grim --
I stood confident with my faith in Him.

My English was poor, so I sought out a man
Who both languages could understand.
He took me to a lawyer who was a lady,
And explained my situation very briefly.

She looked at me and did bluntly say:
"No way will the authorities let you stay."
The battle then was a challenging feat.
They were all against me -- it looked like defeat.

My interpreter refused to translate what I had to say,
But I struggled on in my broken English way.
They wouldn't believe one word I said --
"You've got to go back." 'No, I'd rather be dead!'

I didn't come here to be insulted and treated this way.
My God preformed miracles to get me here today.
My trust is in Him, it is not in you.
Whatever it takes, He will bring me through.

I know I'm in this country to stay.
My all powerful God will work it that way.
"We'll dismiss this case -- Monday, come again.
We'll decide then if you go, or remain."

Now this was a very unusual situation
And over the weekend, the topic of conversation.
On Monday, in a different mind they came:
Brother Cicilee in Canada was allowed to remain.

Against language, man, law and the devil, he won.
Through a series of miracles, God's will was done.
We are happy and with them we firmly stand
To establish God's Kingdom with Him in command.

God gave a wife, with him to stand,
To strengthen, comfort, and hold his hand.
A little son, we also see. Instead of one, he now is three.
A loving, yielded, dedicated, God blessed family.

The Christian Centre presented them to Father
To receive a double portion of His Spirit for this hour.
He is not in a strange land, an orphan, alone
He is flesh of our flesh, and bone of our bone.

In this heavenly body, we are made one.
We girdle them with prayer, God's will to be done.
Our spirits bore witness, they're being sent forth
From the East to the West, and the South and the North.

Canada needs them, the Church does too.
God's arm is not short. There is nothing He can't do.
Knit us Father, Your love, unity and Oneness to know.
Your great grace reserved for this time, let flow.

With all our heart our Lord we praise.
To the hoards of Hell, Thy triumphant Name raise.
Through failure and sin, we confess our defeat.
This is our resurrection day. We stand to our feet.

A Little Swedish Girl

Precious Holy Spirit, help me write this poem
Of this little Swedish lass who had to leave home.
Only fourteen, pretty, small but capable, yet had to go
To work. Why it had to be, I do not know.

Packing was a small job because little did she own.
Tears run down her cheeks because she was leaving home.
The employment office got her a job on an estate in Germany
In a strange land so far from home -- already she was lonely.

The brave little girl she was, didn't want her mother to know
How badly she felt leaving her loved ones and having to go.
She was met by her manager who was shocked at her size,
And doubted her work ability, but got a surprise.

She was so young, but didn't stop until the job was done
And her mild, gentle ways won the heart of each one.
She met a boy. Something clicked on the inside:
"Now that's a real girl. Some day she'll be my bride."

He was an antidote to her loneliness. Love began to grow.
Five years later, she became his bride. He loved her so.
They decided to go to the States to build their home.
Later they would help her parents to come.

In 1891 the only passage was on a small sail boat.
They said goodbye to her people and boarded the float.
No means of communication, if a need should arise.
Only a compass to guide them to the land of paradise.

They were a long way from home when suddenly
A bad wind tossed that ship about unmercifully.
Being on board was surely no joke;
Panic seized them when the propeller broke.

For four long months they were at the mercy of the sea.
No way to steer the boat, they drifted aimlessly.
They had never learned to trust in the Lord
But now their hearts to God they outpoured.

They drifted northward but no land could they see,
Just whales and icebergs threatened their safety.
Beyond all expectation, a bigger ship saw their grief.
The sea more calm now, it came to their relief.

It was unbelievable, they were safe on board.
With one heart they worshipped and praised the Lord.
Great kindness was shown them by the crew on this boat.
They shared what they had with these hungry folk.

They made it safe to the U.S. shore
And praised the Lord over and over.
They purchased a small piece of land to build upon.
A small home and a chicken house, then money was gone.

Little by little the farm did grow.
They bought a few chickens and planted vegetables so
That was the situation when the first son came.
Father kneeling in the hen pen, dedicated him in Jesus'
name.

They worked very hard. Their farm grew and grew.
Then her family came and joined them too.
Her son became a pastor with a compassionate heart.
He built a large Faith Home near Chicago, called Oak Park.

In this home Addie Lowrie and I were invited to live
And received the hospitality they did lovingly give.
Each month there was a beautiful display
Of his mother's embroidery. She helped support in this way.

After I returned from China, a letter came
Telling of a beautiful funeral service in Jesus' Name.
A rejoicing welcome meeting was planned above
For this little Swedish girl -- a child of His love.

Total Freedom for You

Father help me this revelation to put into a poem
For those who have not the privilege to hear this sermon.
Everything happens through faith in God's word,
So I want an explosion of faith in the "Thus saith the Lord".

I cry for Your Kingdom to come and Your will to be done,
That even my lifestyle with You shall be one.
Lift me out of this whirlpool of materialistic, Godless society,
And transplant me into the power of the Word and its reality.

I love a story that Larry tells about a man named Ginks:
Larry is thrilled at what he predominantly thinks:
I believe it. I believe it, yes I believe it. I really do.
So many do not believe God's word is really true.

You really believe it Brother, but what do you believe?
God does bless our finances. If you give, you shall receive.
For fifty years I have believed this. I really do:
God's promises are so abundant and His word is really true.

Larry, just recently married, was sitting in his trailer home.
Suddenly the glory of the Lord filled his small office room.
The Lord said, "Son what would you like Me to give?"
'Wisdom to know You and to teach Your people how to live.'

"You have asked a good thing, a noble request,
And for all your desires, you shall be blessed.
Larry, there are four things My people need to know,
And I'll give you wisdom to teach them everywhere you go."

"They must believe they are the head and not the tail.
What the Word says about finances shall prevail.
They must see debt in the light of Galatians three thirteen.
It is under the curse of the law from which I did redeem."

"They must believe My purpose in them can be done.
Wisdom to get riches, from Me does come.
My wisdom I've laid up -- there is a great supply.
For any who seek it, I shall not deny."

"My blood is the payment to set them free
From the chains of debt, the curse of poverty.
Their lifestyle also they must give to Me,
Before they can reap the harvest abundantly."

"They sowed much but reaped little. They did not believe,
For themselves and by themselves, they could not achieve.
They must live within their means - their daily bread I'll give.
Many of My people beyond their means extravagantly live."

"Here is an example: ten oranges to a man I gave.
Seven for himself, two for tithe and offerings, one to save."
For many years, Larry has carefully followed this pattern,
And God gave him wisdom on how to live and how to spend.

The offerings are for the extra mile of the way.
This is the lifestyle My children must display.
If they keep their priorities straight, they shall be blessed
And I will make a way for them, even through darkness.

'I am dedicated this day to see all of you set free --
Spiritually, emotionally, physically, and financially.
We shall see a supernatural release of God's Spirit outpour.
The Word of God and history tell us -- it is now at the door.'

We must see the Church and Israel in parallel:
Again the Word and history prove this very well.
In 1908 Bricksale started the modern day Zionist movement.
Hungry hearts then cried to God for a Spiritual fulfilment.

Holiness, power, glory, and miracles did the Church adorn.
From all denominations the Pentecostal movement was born
Forty years later, the first time in history, Israel did claim:
The year of Jubilee. This year we shall celebrate it again.

Jubilee means to be joyfully set free.
Likewise the Church is experiencing a glorious reality.
On the day of atonement, there was a mighty shout,
And all the debt-bondaged people were then brought out.

We must be faithful to the precious blood of the Lamb
Delivering us from the curse born in us by Adam.
We are to be happy and rejoicing this is our day of Jubilee.
All our chains have been broken and we are set free.

My eyes have caught the vision. For self I cannot live.
Life is less than useless until my all I give,
To accomplish Your will and purpose with my whole heart,
To be a bright shining light though the days be dark.

Luke 4:18   Isaiah 61:2   Leviticus 25:9
Galations 3:13   Deuteronomy 8:18

Jesus Uses Little Things

The foolish and weak, I have chosen to
Manifest My glory and power, to you.
Your failure and mistakes do not limit Me,
But a repentant, yielded heart, there must be.

For My suffering children, I've prepared a feast,
And there will be restoration for the very least.
I delight to use a little thing;
To Father, it will great glory bring.

I used Saul when he was little in his own eyes,
But when he became famous, then Me he despised.
Saul lost his kingship and fell in disgrace.
I anointed David to reign in his place.

With a jaw bone of an ass in Sampson's hand
Of the Philistines he slew a great band.
Remember how Naman's healing was displayed --
Through the faithful witness of a little maid.

Against a great multitude, a well trained army,
Gideon with three hundred men, set his people free.
He used pitchers, and trumpets, and light,
And put the hosts to death, or to flight.

Elisha shared the lunch given to him,
To feed a large group of hungry men.
With a little boy's lunch, thousands I fed --
To the hungry, sick world, I am the True Bread.

Many times it has been proven what I can do,
So quit doubting, and let Me do it through you.
Your mind and spirit must be under My control,
Then Satan will have no power over your soul.

Stir up the gifts that for you I have obtained,
With My anointing, you will ruin Satan's reign.
There is healing and deliverance, and all you need;
From every bondage of Satan, you can be freed.

If Satan's evil thoughts in your mind you give room,
To that extent, he will possess you and your soul doom.
He will blind you so you will miss this great visitation,
And commandeer you for his work and his condemnation.

We Must Recover It All

Dear Larry preached a sermon that thrilled me to the core,
On how to recover it all and the toughest tests endure.
He gives a Bible road map how to retake what Satan stole:
A direct Word from the Lord Who has all things under control

Now is the time to recover what we've lost to the devil.
God is giving us back what has been spoiled by his evil.
Through Jesus' Blood Covenant, God has recovered all
That Adam sold out to Satan, causing the great fall.

The Bible is a story of recovery for fallen, lost man.
Now His Body is regaining what we lost in Adam.
When we open our heart and invite Jesus to come in
Is when the great plan of recovery in us does begin.

God does have a way to redeem what the spoiler has taken.
There is a time of loss, when faith is severely shaken.
His Word tells us what our attitude should be and what to do
So He can turn the curse into blessing, and our faith renew.

An amazing thing, His Word says He will restore it seven fold
If we live in loving obedience, His power shall take hold,
And cause demons of darkness and unbelieving eyes to see:
Jesus has a people who are walking in His victory.

We've lost friends, love ones, our health, property and gold
And these are the things God plans to restore seven fold.
In a world-wide way, suddenly the unprepared shall see:
There is a God Who through His saints reigns triumphantly.

The contract of this road map 1 Samuel 30 does share:
The most important time in David's life is here.
In First Samuel, David from Saul is fleeing.
In Second Samuel, he isn't running, he is reigning.

61

This is the turning point in David's career:
How he recovered all, is revealed here.
Loss of possession, and loved ones, of David and his men,
Who so grief stricken, had no hope of seeing them again.

They were so overcome and so sick in their soul,
They wanted to stone David. Their emotions had control --
But David encouraged himself in the Lord,
And asked Abiathar to bring the ephod.

Together they sought wisdom in this sad situation
From God, Whom they trusted for their restoration.
"Shall we pursue, or not?" The Lord heard their call.
"Yes, pursue. Without fail you shall recover it all."

David with his men did quickly obey.
They passed by Brook Besor on their way.
Two hundred men were too weak to endure the toil --
David said, wait here 'till we return with the spoil.

They ministered to a sick Egyptian, who was willing to bring
Them to the camp of the victors who were wildly celebrating.
David with his four hundred men soon changed their tune.
All night they cleaned up on them, until the next afternoon.

Four hundred men escaped with nothing, on camels they fled
Then David recovered it all, just as his Lord had said.
Some of David's ungrateful men did selfishly declare:
Our spoil with those two hundred we will not share.

"No, no said David, this evil we cannot do.
The stayers by the stuff, equally share with you."
Here he set his principle on sharing and giving,
Which is the secret of victory, and joyful living.

God works with people by the situations they are in.
David knew he must recover all if he was to win.
In his spirit he knew soon he would be ascending the throne,
But the destruction at Ziglag looked like his end had come.

With the weapons of his warfare he destroyed the foe,
Because he believed what his Lord said, He would do.
There is a truth here God wants us to see:
The weapons He gives us will defeat the enemy.

There are attacks when it seems like the enemy has won.
Our life is seasoned with defeat in the race we have run.
To say we have failed and Jesus cannot restore us again,
Insults the great Calvary victory won through blood and pain

Many know it is our biblical heritage to recover all,
But do not believe He fully conquered their fall.
Due to failures, Satan tells them they have no right to claim
A full recovery in the covenant with Jesus through His name.

Peter thrice denied Jesus, but lost not his soul.
Jesus knew what Peter would do under Spirit control.
Jesus has already prepared for our restoration.
Are we longing for this glorious participation?

This is the hour we must realize the fruits of our claim
And believe for complete recovery in Jesus' name.
When things go from bad to worse, we expect intervention.
The world sees only destruction, but we see resurrection.

This is no time for us to lay down and relax,
But with fasting and praying, arise to face the facts.
God's prophets tell us this year we will sink or swim.
It depends upon our relationship and union with Him.

The greatest protection from evil is love.
Not the flesh-tainted kind, but that which is from above.
It will prevent Satan making a storehouse in our soul to hide
Unforgiveness, unbelief, lying, hate, wrath, greed and pride.

All of these shall inherit the wrath of God in Hell.
There's no word in our language this anguish can tell.
It is so much wiser before our opportunity ends,
To stand on Luke 10:18 and spend eternity with friends.

Epilogue: *We Must Recover It All*

I love David. His whole life is such a pattern for us.
He doesn't think his way out of his troubles;
He doesn't argue his way out of his troubles;

He encourages himself in the Lord;
He praises, he prays and trusts in the Lord.
The joy of the Lord is his strength.
His strength gives him ability to fight.

He learned the power of agreement,
With the use of the ephod or prayer shawl.
He knew the importance of getting
The proper one to be in agreement with you.

He always knew where the enemy was attacking.
The enemy doesn't want us to know
That he is a sneak attacker.

David doesn't let the enemy off with his stealing.
David and his men didn't stop for sleep.
They had just come back from a battle.

They obeyed God. They got after the enemy.
They knew they would get it back.
Two hundred men played out. David didn't discharge them.
He said, 'You wait here. We'll share with you.'
He conquered, he shared, he gave, he restored.

He teaches us that it is of the same importance
To stand by the stuff, and keep passing the ammunition
As it is to be on the battle field -- with Larry,
And the many, many other mighty men of God
Who are trimming the devil, at home and abroad.

There is no more needy field than the one
We are lackadaisically sitting in.
In fact, destruction is coming our way.

The Eagle and The Snake

The majestic eagle is an inspiration to me.
The wisdom God gave him is beautiful to see.
He has but one enemy, which is a big snake;
The eggs and the little ones is what it will take.

Two eyes are watching ·· the snake takes no heed.
Great claws sink into his neck and he goes up in great speed.
The eagle pays no attention to the snake but goes still higher
He knows the squirming snake in the cold will soon tire.

Then limply he falls and dangles down;
Quickly then the eagle zooms toward the ground.
The eagle is going fast now and heading for a rock
The snake is going to get a deathly shock.

The eagle batters it up good, then lets it fall;
He won the battle, but that's not all.
The little ones are saved; they are set free.
Daddy eagle shows them how to get the victory.

That is what Jesus has done for us.
With His heel, Satan's head He did crush.
He won the battle, for us to set free.
Through His omnipotent blood, we have the victory.

A Donkey's Foal Preaches to Me

"All things concerning the Son of Man shall be accomplished
For He shall be delivered unto the Gentiles and be mocked,
And spitefully treated, and spitted upon. They shall scourge
Him and put Him to death; the third day He shall rise again."
Luke 18:31, 32, 33
"That I might know Him, and the power of His resurrection,
And the fellowship of His sufferings,
Being made conformable unto His death."   Philippians 3:10

It was a brand new experience in a totally different way.
No donkey had ever had it, but the one chosen that day.
It had never been broken or trained by man;
Yet it met a need, and fit perfectly into Father's plan.

Jesus told two of His disciples to go, and where
The foal and his mother would be tied there.
The owner will say: 'Why are you taking the colt away?'
Say: "The Master needs him." He'll let him go. And it was so.

They placed their garments on his back.
Jesus mounted, the colt was perfectly relaxed.
No rein or bit was needed to keep him in the way.
He took the right paths, the right gate with no fray.

Children and adults were shouting and praising the Lord,
Waving branches, laying garments before Him on the road.
The colt had no fear or panic within.
The One he carried was the One Who had made him.

But the Pharisees were nervous and very angry.
The One they hated was receiving great glory.
The actions of the colt must have irked them too --
No rein or bit; how could a colt know what to do?

Why did it take Him through the animal gate
That is for the sacrifices? It is all a mistake.
Why did he go to the temple, the house of prayer?
Jesus dismounts, and the colt's mission ends there.

I think he would gallop back to his mother again
And in donkey language, that wonderful trip explain;
Or maybe the disciples returned him in a gentlemanly way;
Perhaps the owner was there enjoying the amazing display.

The One in control was the One Who calmed the sea;
The great Creator, Who made all things for His glory.
In that situation, how could a colt be in perfect control?
We humans contend with a proud, selfish, rebellious soul.

The animals do not have a choice to rebel or obey.
We have an interfering will that fights God's holy way.
Into our hearts Satan has injected all of his evil seed,
And watches over it to thwart what God has decreed.

That was why the Pharisees were mad and wanted to kill
The One Who in them could His great mercies fulfil.
This decision is now ours. Can we truthfully say:
Lord, I'm completely Yours, to do Your will and go Your way.

Why did Jesus not choose the mother?
She probably knew how things should be done.
No, she was not His choice. Instead
He chose the untrained little one.

The foal was an object lesson to the Pharisees.
It wasn't their righteousness Jesus wanted, but humility.
A revelation of this truth we too must know
To fit into His plan, and His virtue show.

Just as the Lord had control over the donkey that day,
If we be willing and obedient, He'll manage us the same way.
I believe that God-chosen foal will be in Heaven too.
I'll slip my arm about his neck and say: "I appreciate you."

Biblical Giving --
A Key to
Blessed Living

Life is much greater than merely making a living.
We conquer our failing economy by biblical giving.
The god of this world is the god of mammon
Who has forged the whole world under his dominion.
The god of mammon strides up the aisle stalking every pew.
The motive of his mission is to bind me and you.

'With living so costly and the taxes so high,
If you give to the Lord's work, you will surely die.'
'Don't attend church services; seek overtime instead,
Another digit to your account is the way to get ahead.
Just turn a deaf ear to the work of the Lord;
All that you have, on yourself must be poured.'

Satan plunges man into great debt -- not caused by need,
But rather covetousness, lust, selfishness and greed.
There is no bottom at all to this endless debt,
Which will end in total loss and hopeless regret.
In the Bible we are told of a vastly different plan:
By giving, you get. It's the word of God, not of man.

"Cast thy bread upon the water, it will yet return to you"
God's children have proven this is experientially true.
All of God's promises we must simply believe,
And in obedience and faith, we expect to receive.
As we put God first in every transaction,
All our needs shall be met with satisfaction.

In Malachi 3:10 God gives us a message that is very plain:
Bring in all the tithes and offerings to be blessed, and gain.
Judges 5:23 declares a bitter curse is upon the head
Of those who come not to 'the help of the Lord' as He said.
Jesus came to Earth and died in great agony and pain,
Committing the preaching of this gospel to man to proclaim.

Man terribly failed in this great decree from the Lord,
Because he trusted in self and not in God's omnipotent word.
God always accomplishes His perfect plan,
So He's sending a powerful restoration to fully equip man.
If we should miss this last great visitation,
We'll lose out on the glorious manifestation.

A Millionaire?

There is a funny story I would like to relate:
It happened after a big fire. At that time I was eight.
Fred Northy was the best teacher our rural school ever had.
He was always in control, even when we children were bad.
One day he decided he would like to see
What his fifty students in the future, wanted to be.

One girl emphatically said, 'I want to be a stenographer'.
I didn't know what that was but wanted to be better than her.
I got it -- and imitated her, 'Oh I want to be a millionaire'.
I thought in my heart, with these poor kids I would share.
'That money will take a long time to get' he said with a smile
'Well I'm young. I guess I'll be around quite awhile.'

There wasn't much quantity or variety in the food we ate.
The clothing we wore was scarcely enough to insulate.
I was twelve when two ladies visited our land of desolation
And in simple reality, shared the story of Salvation.
The first night, I got saved and was so happy inside
Even though comfort and outward adorning were denied.

I found it easy to testify and to pray,
And deep within wanted to be a missionary some day.
I'm so grateful to Jesus for saving me when I was young,
But I have this feeling -- our relationship has just begun.
There were many times I had no idea what to do,
But the Lord in loving mercy made a way through.

Its coming soon, yes very, very soon --
We'll be standing before our beloved Bridegroom.
For our life on earth, He will give His evaluation,
Which will determine forever our eternal destination.
'I know you', or 'I know you not', is what He will say.
Our life passing before us; we'll admit He's just that day.
There is a simple truth that I would like to share:
'If we get to know Him here, He will know us there.'
Jesus lived with motive and purpose of how He would die.
We have selfish motives focused on comfort as time flies by.

Is it to our outward adorning or lifestyle we go in debt to give
Or does our inner man cry for wisdom, in these days to live?
The sides are lining up, our die we now cast.
This great opportunity very soon shall be past.
Don't live beyond your means, eating up tomorrow's bread.
Follow His prayer pattern; your needs He'll meet, as He said.
We'll be accepted in the Beloved, and with Him a joint-heir,
So I can declare to my schoolmates: *I am a millionaire!*
Even though there are things in which I know not what to do,
The Perfect in Knowledge is in me, able to carry me through.

Millionaire Song

I am a millionaire,
With Jesus a joint-heir.
When a need comes marching by,
My faithful Banker is my supply.
All the world's riches belong to Him.
He loves to give, and to share them.
When the last dollar comes into view,
My faithful Banker knows what to do.
He doesn't worry how He'll meet my need.
He just wants to free me from my greed,
And get me in a love-union with Him,
So joyful worship, I can bring.
Now I sing my little song:
He makes right what is all wrong.
He is my Saviour, my Lover, my King.
All I want is to be like Him.

Money and Me

Dear Lord, please take the dollar signs out of my eyes.
Give a revelation of the Source Who my daily needs supplies.
Grant wisdom how this money is to be spent.
I understand You do not want me to be extravagant.

Give me wisdom even in the food I buy.
To be fully obedient to Your leading, and not my eye.
My whole lifestyle with You must be in harmony,
Then I shall not need to worry about shortage of money.

A few small fish and a little bread was a small boy's food.
He gave all to Jesus Who blessed it and fed a big crowd.
Now gather up the fragments, our dear Lord did say,
Each of the twelve had a full basket to enjoy along the way.

To feed the Israelis God abundantly did provide
So that great multitude of people were daily satisfied.
Moses said: get up early and gather according to your need.
If you over gather, it will stink, because of your greed.

There is a point here God wants me to see
The trend of my flesh, by nature is to be greedy.
Now watch when a pie by you is passed --
The big pieces go first and the small ones last.

The Chinese say a straw on the wall tells which way the wind
blows. Likewise little traits clearly my character shows.
Now Jesus' nature in me, makes me love to share,
Not just grab for myself, and for the needs of others not care.

I will cast my bread upon the water; not worry what shall be.
In due time with big interest my Lord will send it back to me.
Lord I do not want to sow my seed sparingly
Because my eternal harvest will be accordingly.

Give With A Purpose

II Corinthians 9: 7, 10

The Word tells me, my giving is a seed to multiply,
And my daily food it will supply.
My garden shall flourish in productiveness;
And will also increase my righteousness.

I must have an eternal purpose in my giving
Which is in my heart; not just my thinking.
It is an important part of joyful worship declares verse seven,
If we want to reap a harvest, as the promise is given.

To this great truth, if I do not take heed;
The devil will surely devour my seed.
We must give expecting, with eternity's values in view.
Souls for whom Christ died depend on me and you.

Brother Duplantis says, the devil we must resist;
If we don't inevitably, him, we will assist.
Giving is the hinge, on which it will swing.
We must name our purpose, and with joy do our giving.

God's prophets tell us: don't hoard your money;
No way can it guarantee you security.
Things happen so suddenly -- in just one day
All of your money could be swept away.

Do we want to be happy and this sick world bless?
Be a cheerful giver and we'll increase our righteousness.
If we keep Jesus forever in our eye,
Our every need He will supply.

When calamity strikes and folk have to flee;
I've wondered what I would do, if it were me.
In the latter days, you shall consider it perfectly.
Declares the prophet Jeremiah in chapter thirty.

A deluge of filth is bathing our nation.
Satan is sweeping it into his condemnation.
We dare not in the god of mammon trust;
Or we will lose out on the restoration God has for us.

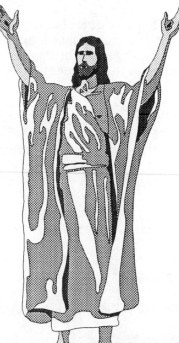

He Is Our Sufficiency

Jesus is my Healer, constant comfort and guide.
He is my Banker, my daily needs are supplied.
This abundant Supplier wants me to be wise
And keep the will of His Kingdom before mine eyes.

He promises to meet all of my daily need.
To go in debt, live above my means, denotes greed.
He doesn't want me to eat up tomorrow's bread
But to declare His word, and believe what He said.

I choose His leading; His saints I love to meet;
He's making us one in the Father, His plan to complete.
The distress that suddenly confronts us, is as He's planned.
No matter what package they come in, they're in His hand.

We may be wounded, and our situations be dark.
Remember it's in His hand, and of His plan, a vital part.
He knows how to wreak our ship upon His grace,
To refine us, and make all things fall into place.

73

He has a special purpose and plan for each one,
So we rejoice in our circumstances, for His will to be done.
Trials and testings are for our promotion, I heard one say,
And Jesus gathers up the fragments; nothing goes astray.

Jesus is our Healer, and knows the pressure it will take,
To bring forth a spotless trophy, that only He can make.
Alone He bore the curse, forsaken in agony and pain,
That for us, this glorious victory, He could obtain.

To us, the cross is a decision, dedication, oneness and love,
Complete submission to Kingdom rule from Father above.
It'll mean stripping off our plumage, but His will we'll take,
And from our ashes, a nugget of pure gold He will make.

The gate is so small that we must enter in;
No room for big bundles of self pity, pride and sin.
To some, the cross is a stumbling block which they hate;
Such a crossing out of the flesh life, they just can't take.

So they become vessels of dishonour, doomed to die
In an eternal Hell, where they'll regretfully cry:
'If only I had listened and His word faithfully obeyed,
The glory of Heaven with me would have stayed.'

In the eternal anguish which is beyond all words or control,
To spend eternity with the deceiver and destroyer of the soul
There will be no way then, to change what has been done.
Now is the time to surrender all, and to Jesus come.

There is little time left, this decision to make
Else, of His great wrath on all sin, we'll partake.
"Follow Me" are the words at this hour, we must hear;
Receive love, joy, grace and faith, void of all fear.

Soon there shall be a shout from the portals on high.
The black clouds will roll back and leave a clear sky.
The Bride with her Lover united shall be,
In a glorified joint reign throughout eternity.

74

Let Us Take Inventory

Father I ask Thee to take this inventory with me.
I want to know how my life lines up with Thee.
Your Word tells me my flesh is corrupt, polluted with sin,
And into Your holy presence, it could not stand to enter in.

Your ways and words to my fleshly thinking are foolishness.
If Your purpose is my living they're power and righteousness
In Galatians 5: 19 to 21, I see a bad list that's buried in me,
And these are the roots that produce my carnality.

I dare not give room for them to grow in my soul.
They feed on demonic power, and will take control.
I should not read the Word, for a sermon for you:
But to search my own heart about the things I say and do.

In 1 Corinthians 1: 27 Paul gives to us an amazing key.
He chose the weak and despised, so flesh could not glory.
He wants to cleanse and deliver us from bondage and sin,
And give a new heart, with a sole purpose to glorify Him.

God wants to have a Body, not a basket case:
Each one doing his part, is God's plan of grace.
As Children of Faith our eyes are fixed on God,
We stand triumphant, through His omnipotent Blood.
                                        Revelation 12:11
We are to God a Flavour of Christ, that is very sweet,
And He has planned for us, absolutely no defeat.
The climax of the ages is God's total restoration:
His Trophy shall be exhibited in holy demonstration.

This is the greatest company the world shall ever see:
His chosen shall be brought forth in perfect unity.
To be in this selection takes a surrendered heart;
Our motive, just Jesus, and from all sin to depart.

Sin is sweet in the mouth, but the poison of asps within.
Many names will be blotted out because of love for their sin.
God will have a people of purity and revelation,
With which He will finish His work in this generation.

A God Who Hears Your Prayer

Thou who hearest prayer, we come to Thee.
Your precious blood has purged all our iniquity.
Thou art our Help and sure Anchor of our soul,
And all of these testings are under Your control.

My lips shall praise Thee for Thy loving kindness,
Which so sweetly delivers from all loneliness.
My heart longs to see Thy power and glory,
Thou who hearest prayer, we come to Thee.

Thy precious blood avails for my hip, my back and my head,
And I am refreshed as I remember Thee upon my bed.
You temper every wind that blows,
And where our paths lead, Your eye also goes.

Thou art the strength of my heart, my loins and my feet,
Through Thine atoning blood, I am complete.
Thou art the strong tower in whom I can hide;
Thou art the living vine in Whom I can abide.

I thank You, dear Lord, Your provision is so complete;
There is no reason at all why I should suffer defeat.
Make me alert and wise to see
Just how Satan is trying to manipulate me.

He uses seven deadly sins to contaminate the soul,
And hinders enjoying our Salvation to the full.
Pride, greed, envy, wrath, sloth, lust and gluttony;
These make up an evil package of carnality.

Make me alert these evils to see,
And humbly confess them, dear Lord to Thee;
So Your precious blood can cleanse them away,
And keep me free as in faith I pray.

There are so many loved ones, I long to sustain,
That a fruitful branch in the vine, they will remain.
Thou who hearest prayer, to Thee I come,
That Your name be glorified, and Your will be done.

76

Be Blessed By Father's Name

John 17:6, 26

May His beautiful Spirit rejuvenate your soul.
Jehovah-Yahweh wants you to give Him control.
Jehovah-Iohim is with you there,
The Great Creator Who answers prayer.

Jehovah-Ishadai is all sufficient.
Jehovah-Issi in you is the Omnipotent.
Jehovah-Epheka is your Health.
Jehovah-Jireh is your Wealth.

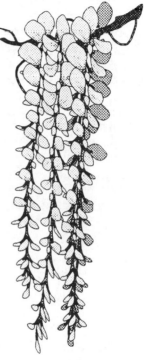

There is such a big God abiding in me.
My limitations do not matter, you see.
I felt His love, and it was so sweet.
I would like to hug and kiss His feet.

You hug my Body, and let love flow free.
When you hug Mine, you are hugging Me.
Give to those I love, and you give to Me.
I miss nothing. I give back abundantly.

The more you give to others,
The more I can pour into thee,
And fulfil in you My joy and glory,
Which automatically returns to Me.

Your capacity shall then increase.
Keep expecting this great release.
Keep reading My word with prayer.
What I give you, with others share.

Lord, Your sweet presence, I appreciate.
My thirsty soul, please do saturate;
So Your Holy Spirit may have His way,
And these lips say what You want to say.

To the hurting ones, Your faith impart;
And restore the fallen with a clean heart.
I love you Jesus. You are my Elohim.
Create a light in me that does not dim.

The Spirit of Jesus is For Us

There is an abundant supply of Jesus' Spirit for us.
We receive it from God in Whom we trust.
It is excellent, fruitful and very sincere,
Filled with glory and praise, which to God is most dear.

If the word as from God, not man, we receive,
It will work effectively in us, if we believe.
We must see all His Spirit to us He has given
By His precious promises, His nature in us is woven.

The world will admit, with Jesus we have been
When His righteousness, oneness and love are seen.
As we see it's all ours through the shedding of His blood,
It will fill us with joy and rejoicing in our wonderful Lord.

We turn a deaf ear to all of Satan's lies
And without a doubt, know God's Word to us applies.
The old Adam, we put off and the Word we confess,
And put on the new Adam, and manifest His righteousness.

Like it worked in Jesus, it will also work in us,
If we receive and believe without striving or fuss.
We must be filled with praise to glorify our Lord
And realize it is all in the blood, that for us was outpoured.

Jesus' Spirit will present the Bride without spot or blemish
And the great plan of God, quickly shall be finished;
So in us can be, this complete fulfilment of His will,
And for this vision, we must set ourselves like steel.

Reconciliation with forgiveness, there must be.
This is what Jesus has purchased for me.
If I give myself to the truth expressed here,
I will fulfil His will in Godly fear.

United With Jesus

I'm united with Jesus at Calvary.
He became my curse to set me free.
Every bondage He broke, He broke for me.
He became my curse and now I am free.

I am so happy in Jesus Whom I adore.
His blessings run after me more and more.
There is joy and rejoicing deep inside.
I'm His blood-bought treasure, His future Bride.

I'm a tree planted by His river.
Down go my roots for a drink from the Giver.
My leaves are green and no heat do I see,
And fruit for His glory grows abundantly.

I'm yet far from what You want me to be:
A helper to those whose path is rough and stony.
Many times I missed You dear Lord.
I thank You for the times I passed beneath Your rod.

I love You Lord. You were so patient with a slow learner,
So blind to what hindered being a spiritual discerner.
Father I'm old now, my great longing is to see
My loved ones brought into harmony with Thee.

Let them feel the sweetness of Your matchless grace.
And Father's Love so powerful against trials they'll face.
You are peace in the midst of the raging storm of today,
A refuge, a fortress, a high tower, a hiding place and stay.

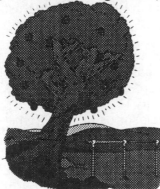

The Vine and the Branch   John 15: 1,2

"I am the true Vine, and My Father is the Husbandman.
Every branch in Me that beareth not fruit, He taketh away;
Every branch in Me that beareth fruit,
He purgeth it that it may bring forth more fruit."

I am a branch in the Vine, a branch in the Vine.
He grafted me in, so I am His, and He is mine.
Now His life and love can in me flow
Causing His fruit to abundantly grow.

As I drink in of His love, I become filled with God's fullness
And automatically produce His fruits of righteousness.
In fruits of righteousness, the Husbandman is glorified
And to produce this fruit, the flesh must be crucified.

No matter how very hard my flesh may try,
The fruit will only wither, shrivel and die.
Eventually I will suffer very great loss
If I continually shun the death of the cross.

When you see an orchard where fruit in abundance grows,
It testifies the vine dresser, his job thoroughly knows.
He prunes and purges with careful skill
To make each branch bring forth his will.

God's motive is that not some, but much fruit will appear.
He treasures each one; to Him it is very dear.
The life is His, the fruit is His, but the reward He gives to us -
If only our flesh we forsake and in Him we wholly trust.

Our glorious Lord will be unto us a broad stream
On which no galley boat or gallant ship shall be seen.
The 'galley' is our efforts, the 'gallant' our pride;
Neither of these two can the Lord abide.   Isaiah 33:21

His unlimited supply is available for us to draw from.
It eclipses whatever degenerate flesh could have done;
So let us get real hungry and whet up our appetite
Just keep drinking in of Jesus and we'll come out alright.
80

Prayer Answered

I want to write a poem today.
Precious Holy Spirit tell me what to say.
You know I am old, my hair is turning white,
And one look would tell You, I am no good to fight.

In the word something illumined my sight --
A dry, old stick yielded fruit in one night.
From whence did it come, this new life release?
How do I appropriate it? Do tell me please.

There is a joyful stirring deep inside;
"Lord, I long to see You and be part of Your Bride."
"My Bride over all Hell shall prevail.
Satan's mighty onslaughts, She shall curtail."

"This glorious victory to display
It is not in you to know the way;
But it is in Me, My purpose I'll carry through
And do it through vessels, even like you."

"If you humbly repent and commit your all to Me
From carnal flesh, I'll set you free.
Fear, feeling and thinking are the fruits of the soul
That will plunge into dreadful darkness if allowed control.

Faith needs no sight or feeling; It simply trusts in My Word
Which guarantees victory, with your eyes fixed on your Lord."
"There is nothing too hard for Me to do;
And if there's no way at all, I can make one for you."

There is a battle in the heavenlies human eyes cannot see;
But the Lord and His angels are in place to finish quickly.
There are great quakes, floods, famines, shedding of blood;
Because God is sweeping the world with His judicial flood.

The whole world shall see God's power, grace and glory.
Those who refuse to repent shall end in grief for eternity.
Those who dedicate themselves and yield to Him
Shall shine as the stars and not grow dim.

81

The Bride shall be cleansed, faithful and true;
A replica of Jesus, and His work shall do.
The eyes of the world shall be opened wide.
Terror shall grip them -- the Lord they denied.

Repent, repent, God's faithful servants cry:
God's great wrath is now upon us. Why do you die?
Turn ye, turn ye. Seek the Lord with all of your heart.
He'll be your Light, Comfort and Refuge in the darkest dark.

The battle is not over. We must fight until we die,
And be gloriously united with Christ in the sky.
It will be worth it all, we will regret no pain.
We will be one with Jesus in His eternal reign.

———————— ••◖●◗•• ————————

It Pays to Read the Word

The mighty God, even the Lord hath spoken, and called the
earth from the rising of the sun, to the going down thereof.
                                             Psalms 50: 1
Blessed is the man that feareth the Lord
And delighteth greatly in His written word.
Of His divine nature, we through His promises may partake,
And the more our inner man like Him, shall take shape.

His word hidden in our heart will keep us from sin,
And will enrich our praise and worship of Him.
Its the best way to get intimate with our loving Lord;
We get to know Him through His written word.

In the new covenant we appreciate what His blood has done;
Regardless of our situation there's deliverance for each one.
He sanctified Himself unto the death of the cross;
That through His shed blood, He can sanctify us.

If I commit my all to Him, then He will release
His faith and power that will fit me for His masterpiece.
My emotions, will, and desire shall be --
As His will is done in Heaven, do also in me.

82

So don't limit God. There is nothing He cannot do.
He can work out His fruitful plan in you.
Its so thrilling to be alive in this closing day
And see God working in such a wonderful way.

If you long for His mercies, in you to fulfil,
Believe the steps that you take now, are in His will.
He'll pour out His Spirit and His word you'll know --
It will be clear which way you should go.

His Word in Our Mouth   Psalms 17:3

I am purposed my mouth shall not transgress
In voicing the devil's words of unrighteousness.
If I speak his words I perform his actions --
This gives him great, wicked satisfaction.

"Why do negative words automatically come out?"
'My word isn't in your mouth to put them to route.'
'If you carefully listen to what I have to say,
My glorious victory can be yours today.'

"Tell me, how do I do this terrible thing?"
'By doing what you want to do and loitering.
The devil finds work for idle hands to do.
He is very alert, a demonic eye always is on you.'

'Don't get consumed by doing your own thing.
A terrible, eternal reward it will surely bring.'
"What about all my work which I must do?"
'What about all My promises I've given you?'

'I'm not against work except the work of the devil
Who is using your circumstances to bring forth his evil.
Didn't I tell you to acknowledge Me in all your way?
I'll give wisdom but you must pay attention to what I say.'

'Tithes and offerings, in good measure, give cheerfully
And expect Me to bless you abundantly.'
"I am in a dilemma. I don't even have enough."
'You trust your money, not My word in your mouth.'

'I was in the flesh and had a great hard work to do.
Early I was in Father's presence, to carry Me through.'
"How do I know what I am supposed to say?"
'Rely on the Holy Spirit, in you He knows the way.'

'I know your situations and you have no way out.
Decisions give to Me, I'll turn the curse about.
Repent, seek Me in the midst of failure, sickness and doubt.
Receive My peace, freedom will come with your shout.'

'You've no idea of the blessings, if you walk in My way.
Get up early to seek Me, hear Me, and carefully obey.
The times ahead will be desperately, desperately rough.
Taking for granted you know My word and way isn't enough.'

'I have many today who are totally abandoned to Me.
They know My joy and are experiencing My glory.
Obediently listen, let this be your story to share;
So awake and repent, you must be clean My glory to bear.'

His Word is His Bond --My Word is My Bond

"Simon Peter, a servant and apostle of Jesus Christ, To them
that have obtained like precious faith with us through the
righteousness of God and our Saviour Jesus Christ. Grace
and peace be multiplied to you through the knowledge of
God and our Saviour Jesus Christ according as He hath
given us *all things* that pertain unto life and godliness,
through the knowledge of Him that called us to glory and
virtue. Whereby are given unto us exceeding great and
precious promises; That by these we might be partakers of
the divine nature, Having escaped the corruption that is in
the world through lust."   II Peter 1: 1-4

In His likeness, He created me.
Now He desires, me like Him to be.
Because of rebellion, I was born in sin
With Satan's nature planted within.

His word says 'no sin can enter Heaven'
My carnality can produce only sin-leaven.
Through the blood covenant, I've been adopted to God.
He quickened my dead spirit through His word.

His character, like seed was planted within
But it must be developed to make me like Him.
Only the word can make this seed grow
And my wonderful Lord, to get to know.

If I believe His word, it will work effectively
And all of my needs, He will meet abundantly.
If in my circumstances, His word stands the test,
My words also shall bear His righteousness.

Trials and testings are to enlarge my capacity,
And prepare me to hold more of His glory
Then in me He can accomplish His plan
And in the hard places, give grace to stand.

If I grow, I go forward.
If I don't grow, I go backward.
My light then becomes darkness
And I establish my self-righteousness.

It is easy to be side-tracked by worldly fun
And blinded to the agonies that are to come.
When God's wrath is being outpoured
A greater grace needs be endowed.

Our spirit, soul, and body must be cleansed from sin
Because we need God's holiness, in these days to win.
Bitter and sweet water, in us cannot be.
We must be holy to stand His glory.

In God's wisdom, He gave me a will.
His will leads to Heaven, and mine, to Hell.
My choices mould my character, determine my destiny.
Only Jesus can make me the woman He wants me to be.

Words mean nothing in the world today,
But they're either life or death, Solomon did say.
God's word is His bond, it never can fail.
If our word is our bond, it shall prevail.

Daniel's Vision

Daniel had a vision he could not understand 1
What he was seeing, he could not comprehend. 2
He heard one saint ask another, how long shall it be --
The desolation of this host and of the sanctuary?

Two thousand and 300 days was the reply,
Then shall the sanctuary be cleansed thereby. 3
Daniel didn't know what this conversation meant
Until Gabriel was called and unto Daniel was sent.

He fell face down and went into a deep sleep because of fear,
But every word Gabriel said, he could clearly hear.
He touched him -- he was strengthened and sat up
While Gabriel explained to him this last bitter cup.

I'll make you know and cause you to see
What the appointed desolation of the end time shall be:
In the latter time transgressors shall come to the full
And a fierce king shall stand up and take control.

With satanic power and wisdom he'll prosper wonderfully,
Destroying God's people who are holy and mighty.
Then against the Prince of princes he shall boldly stand,
But he shall be broken to pieces without a hand.

Daniel fainted when he was permitted to see
The horrors of the end time and what shall be.
He was astonished and sick at the vision that day
And was unable to serve in his usual way.
Regardless of feelings, he rose up in faithfulness
And went about performing the king's business.

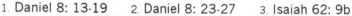

1. Daniel 8: 13-19   2. Daniel 8: 23-27   3. Isaiah 62: 9b

Let God's Word Do the Talking

The word of God is telling me
If I have a wicked heart of unbelief, or of faith and equity
My heart really wants to do God's will
And according to His Word, it can His purpose fulfill

A portion of Jesus' faith God has given me.
Hebrews 12: 2 says He is the Author and Finisher of it
Which is accomplished by His Word and Spirit.
United with that faith is His joy, which by He
In victory could beat the agonies of Calvary.

John 17: 13 says that very joy He spake into me
Brings forth His oneness and victory.
This precious faith I must value carefully.
Its a deciding factor in my eternal destiny.
A little seed of this faith, we can attain
To remove our mountains in Jesus' name.

Peter tells us of a daily spiritual addition
That will bring about our transformation.
The first chapter of second Peter gives an important clue
To make us victorious and His will to do.

In verse 5 this addition brings forth a great increase
And the blessings of God it will freely release:
Add to your faith virtue, that virtue is God;
As we add Him we get to know Him, and love His Word.

Add to virtue knowledge, to knowledge temperance,
To temperance patience, to patience Godliness, to
Godliness brotherly kindness, to brotherly kindness charity
And if these things abound in me they make me
That I will neither be barren nor unfruitful in the
Knowledge of Christ. If I lack these things, I am blind
With no eternal vision, and my light becomes darkness.

Besides this I must be diligent to know my calling.
These are the things that will keep me from falling.
An entrance shall be ministered unto me abundantly
Into the everlasting kingdom of
Our Lord and Saviour, Jesus Christ.

If I do not appropriate God's great provision
Automatically I will make a negative decision.
Job expresses it this way in chapter 21: 14, he says:
God depart from us we desire not the knowledge of Thy ways

Jeremiah 17: 5 says: cursed be the man who trusts
In man and makes the arm of flesh His stay;
He will depart from the Lord and go His own way,
In the imagination of his evil heart, and will not listen to Me."

Paul gives a warning in Hebrews chapter 12 verse 3:
Take heed lest an evil heart of unbelief be in me
And I depart from the living God who can set me free.
Then my heart becomes hardened so I cannot hear
The sweet words of Jesus that dispel all fear.

It takes diligence to keep these truths growing
But they will, if His truth in our spirit we keep sowing.
Our delightful Lord we will get to know
His joy and peace like a river will flow
It will purify the inner man
To make it ready for the glory God has planned.
The overflowing anointing of the Spirit
He has declared it and He is doing it.

What I feed my spirit my tongue tells the tale --
To my words I must take careful inventory
To be ready for the manifestation of His glory.
If we could see what awaits us we'd say: Its worth it all.
Let us clean up on the flesh words and answer God's call.
A deadly battle against the flesh it will take
We will want God, or Him we will forsake.

The greater our faithfulness, the greater our anointing
The greater our anointing, the greater our responsibility
Which needs a greater dedication, says Benny Hinn.
What God gives us is to be used for service --
It is not for us to be worshipped.

"According as His divine power hath given unto us
All things that pertain to life and Godliness, through the
Knowledge of Him Who hath called us to glory and virtue."
2 Peter 1: 3

God's Way to Live According to Proverbs

This way works because it is God's plan.
He made it simple so we could understand.
Through His goodness He brought us into this transaction,
Into a fruitful, happy life of healthy satisfaction.

The way to the heart is by the eyes and the ears.
Faith, patience and love protect it from demonic fears.
Faith need only God's word; patience hangs on in the testing;
And the love of Jesus enables us, in Him to keep resting.

Honour God by giving Him all you are.
He'll honour you by giving you all He is.
Now He is your partner, so make His business your business.
He will make your business His business, and He never fails.

What all does it take to get in on this deal?
You just walk by faith and not by the feel.
Receive the Word's correction and function in His way,
Refuse natural wisdom, and fleshly words don't say.

It takes a revelation to get wisdom and understanding.
He is smarter than you so let Him do the planning.
When you cross out your ways, this is discretion,
Then Jesus will take over and give you His direction.

What He gives, guard with diligent equity.
He'll flood your soul with joyful tranquillity.
If we keep the wrong stuff in our heart, we'll see
There'll be a sudden calamity with no remedy. 1

A backslidden heart with his own ways will fill. 2
He will rage against God, and not do His will.
The words that he speaks are like the piercing of a sword.
His ways are so perverse, he frets against the Lord. 3

The tongue has the power to live or to die.
The words that he speaks come from his spirit supply. 4
His pride to the Lord is an abomination. 5
Its destination is destruction and condemnation. 6

To have no control over the spirit is like an unwalled city. 7
Destruction like a whirlwind will come with no pity 8
To set aside God's counsel and reject His correction 9
Is to eat the fruit of the flesh which is eternal rejection. 10

Go from the presence of an evil man --
With a raging man do not go
Lest you learn his ways and ensnare thy soul.
A man of wrath shall surely suffer great pain. 11
He troubleth his house, who is greedy to get gain. 12

My son despise not your mother when she is old. 13
Give Me your heart and My ways behold. 14
Your Redeemer is mighty. He will plead your case. 15
He preserveth the way of His saints with His grace. 16

I will make you to know the Word's certainty 17
That you can enforce with His authority. 18
That is the weapon that will put Satan to flight; 19
And that is the weapon with which we fight. 20, 21

---

1. Proverbs 6:15   2. Proverbs 14:14   3. Proverbs 19:3
4. Proverbs 18:21a 5. Proverbs 16:5   6. Proverbs 16:18
7. Proverbs 25:28   8. Proverbs 1:27   9. Proverbs 1:25
10. Proverbs 1:31   11. Proverbs 19:19a 12. Proverbs 15:27
13. Proverbs 23:22 14. Proverbs 23:26   15. Proverbs 23:11
16. Proverbs 2:8   17. Proverbs 22:21   18. Proverbs 29:2a
19. Proverbs 28:1   20. Hebrews 4:12   21. Ephesians 6:16

Speeches of Wisdom   (Author Unknown)

It isn't hard to make a mountain out of a mole hill.
Just add a little dirt.
                              Proverbs 12: 14
A critical spirit is like poison ivy.
It only takes a little contact to spread its poison.
                              I Timothy 2: 16
A minute of thought is worth more
Than an hour of talk.
                              Psalms 141: 3
Every job is a self portrait of the one who does it.
Autograph your work with excellence.
                              Proverbs 31: 29
Stack every bit of criticism
Between two layers of praise.
                              Psalms 27: 2
You cannot do a kindness too soon because you never know
How soon it will be too late.
                              Hebrews 3: 13
Life is like a coin. You can spend it how you like,
But you can only spend it once.
                              James 4: 14
Be like a postage stamp.
Stick to one thing until you get there.
                              1 Corinthians 15: 58
Sow courtesy, and you will reap friendship.
Sow friendship, and you will reap love.
                              Galations 6: 7 - 9
Worry is like a rocking chair.
It gives you something to do, but gets you nowhere.

Look around you, and you will be distressed.
Look within you, and you will be depressed.
Look to Jesus, and you will be at rest.
                              Psalms 120: 1
There is no greater love than the love
That hangs on when there is nothing to hold on to.
                              I Corinthians 13: 8
Daily prayers diminish your cares.
                              1 Corinthians 15: 58
It's not what we say we have,
It's having what we say.
                              Mark 11: 24

What Colossians Speaks to Me

Someone told me to read this book thirty times.
It would revolutionize the thoughts of my mind.
I asked Father to let these words jump into my soul,
And keep the members of this clay house under control.

Paul prayed: Father and Lord Jesus Christ, for me to bless,
With peace and the Word of Truth to bring forth fruitfulness.
A love for all saints, in the spirit of revelation,
Of the grace of God, to walk worthy of Him in this generation

Be filled with wisdom, spiritual understanding and trust,
That the knowledge of God will be increasing in us.
New strength to gain as He releases His glorious power.
I need that fresh anointing to stand in this hour.

With a grateful heart of praise and thanks giving to Father
For the blood bought union with Christ, our elder Brother.
We're translated from darkness into the Kingdom of His Son,
Complete forgiveness through His blood, this victory won.

It pleased the Father, in Him, all His fullness should dwell.
Through His death, all things to Himself, he could reconcile.
So I don't have to give up; I don't have to give in
To the bondage of Satan, through my selfishness and sin.

We have an everlasting, unchanging, unlimited source.
He is able through the weak, to manifest His divine force.
With assurance and understanding, knit together in love,
And steadfast in faith in His Kingdom order above.

Paul tells us be careful of those who walk not in God's ways,
And be aware of the body of sin Satan will try to raise.
All our carnality we've sentenced to the cross,
Declaring the resurrection power over sin and dross.

Every negative force was nailed to the cross and taken away.
Over all the power of Satan, He triumphed gloriously.
He did it for the "Body", the Church, His bride,
So we can be complete in Jesus the crucified.

One time our carnal culture we did manifest,
But now with the heavenly culture, we are blest.
We have put off old Adam with his deeds,
And put on the New Adam Who meets all our needs.

We are members of His Body in a particular place,
To minister in love to others with songs of grace.
Whatever we do, do it for God not man:
Man will surely forget us, but God never can.

Pray for the Body of Christ, she will mightily manifest,
All the will of God, in perfect completeness.
Let her speech be with grace so she can
In love and wisdom of God, answer every man.

Make us ministers according to Your dispensation,
And bring forth fulfilment of Your Word in this generation.
Let us experience the richness of Your glory,
To present to all this transforming Life story.

To be part of His Bride, needs a divine revelation.
It exceeds the stretch of my human imagination.
We'll be presented to Father in great glory and grace,
Each member receiving our Lover's embrace.

I have told my Lord I just can't understand.
To be in such an honoured, loved group, I can't comprehend.
I want to be with those who cry for their Lover to come.
Spotless and ready for such a fulfilment in our eternal home.

If I set my affections on things above,
And fill my heart with the riches of His Word and love.
His will to be my constant desire and delight.
I'll hear the trumpet and be gone at the speed of light.

Pray Reading
Some Psalms

I shall not die but live and declare the works of the Lord 1
And in my God shall I praise His omnipotent word. 2
Thou hast delivered me from death to walk before the living
And wave the banner of Truth which Thou hast given. 3

Of Thy power and mercy aloud shall I sing 4
Even in the time You show me a very hard thing. 5
In the day of trouble, my Defence and Refuge shalt Thou be.
By Your right hand deliver Your Beloved, save and set free. 6

Though Thou makest the Earth to tremble and shake 7
The wine of astonishment we need not take. 8
As I trust in Him and pour out my heart, I'll see 9
At all times God shall be a refuge for me.

Through our God we shall do valiantly 10
For He it is that shall tread down our enemy.
He is the God of my salvation and my glory, 11
The Rock of my strength and refuge is He.

Return, we beseech Thee, Oh God and visit this vine 12
That we go not back but call on the name which is Thine. 13
Those that fear Thee, whether great or small 14
Keep Thou their feet that they shall not fall. 15

Let the righteous be glad and exceedingly rejoice 16
And bless our God for His wise choice 17
Let all those that seek Thee be glad in Thee
And magnify the God of our salvation continually. 18

We shall be glad and in His righteousness glory 19
That all the Earth shall sing and worship Thee 20
And observe how God leads His sons in this age of grace
Through fire and water, but into a wealthy place. 21

Let my mouth be filled with praise and bless His name. 22
And let the whole world be filled with His glory. Amen. 23
That this generation also might see
Thy power to every one throughout eternity. 24

I am old now and my hair is grey 25
But quicken Thou me in Thy way.
Until the day of Thy power in the beauty of holiness 26
When Thou shalt cut short Your work in righteousness. 27

Thou shalt increase and comfort me on every side. 28
Keep me in the company of the Lamb's spotless Bride. 29
Blessed be the God who doeth wondrously 30
May the whole earth be filled with His power and glory. 31

---

1. Psalms 118:17	2. Psalms 56:13	3. Psalms 60:4
4. Psalms 59:16	5. Psalms 60:3	6. Psalms 60:5
7. Psalms 60:2	8. Psalms 60:3	9. Psalms 62:8
10. Psalms 60:12	11. Psalms 62:7	12. Psalms 80:14
13. Psalms 80:18	14. Psalms 115:13	15. Psalms 56:13
16. Psalms 68:3	17. Psalms 66:12	18. Psalms 70:4
19. Psalms 64:10	20. Psalms 66:4	21. Psalms 66:12
22. Psalms 71:8	23. Psalms 72:19	24. Psalms 71:18
25. Psalms 71:18	26. Psalms 110:3a	27. Romans 9:28
28. Psalms 71:21	29. Revelation 19:7	30. Psalms 72:18
31. Psalms 72:19		

The Soil
and the Seed
Mark 4: 24

I'd like to write a poem on Mark chapter four.
The Holy Spirit illuminated it to me as ne'er before.
Our hearts are the garden of the Lord.
We are the earth in which He sows His word.

The soil of our heart determines the fruit we bear.
Our Lord makes four divisions, this truth to share:
The first three picture failure and defeat.
The good soil pictures a victory complete.

The difference in soil is what we must see.
What we watch, hear, and say, matters for eternity.
The soil texture determines our fruitfulness.
The negative is flesh works. The positive His righteousness.

To have good soil is made very clear:
It depends on His word, and how we hear.
The value we place on God's word determines our destiny.
If we suffer defeat, we are bound in iniquity.

The negatives say: *Can God* the impossible do?
The positives say: Yes, *God can*, and will bring me through.
Why does God's eye go through the Earth? He's searching for
A people who believe Him and open wide their heart's door.

The negative produces a lifeless religion.
The positive, with Christ has a glorious union.
They take the limits off Jesus. He takes the limits off them.
His engrafted word transforms their soul with blessing.

We can't take a sinful heart to Heaven.
It must be cleansed and forgiven.
Some say they could not fit into the holiness of Heaven
But are not bad enough for Hell: Is there a third place given?

Jesus in great agony took our punishment to set us free.
If we bypass Him, it will be Hell for eternity.
We must listen to the omnipotent word from Heaven.
To those who hear, more shall be given.

The deceitfulness of riches, and lusts, end in destruction.
No hope, no way out -- an eternal agony beyond imagination.
Acquaint now yourself with Him, and blessed be.
Then you will enjoy Him throughout eternity.

Why Pray

I heard a tape sermon yesterday which blessed my soul
And brought forth a cry: Dear Father please take full control.
'Father in Heaven, hallowed be Thy name, most Holy One
As Your will is performed there, now let it in me be done.'

Bob Willkite was preaching. His subject was 'Why Pray'.
Tremendous truths were brought forth in a beautiful way.
'Dear Father, let this light now shine through me,
And let these thoughts flow in poetical simplicity.

Bob was a young man just 18 years old.
He was in the army and far from Father's fold.
In his mother's church was a wailing wall of prayer.
On it the unsaved family pictures were placed there.

The whole church took up the burden and found their place
At that wall 'till each picture experienced God's saving grace.
It was then placed on the other wall called 'The Victory side'
Then there was great rejoicing as Jesus' blood was reapplied

One night his mum with a sad broken heart came in.
Beloved ones pray, my dear Bob is sinking deep in sin.
In one accord they each obediently went.
The time in earnest prevailing prayer was spent.

Something suddenly happened to Bob when he sat to eat.
A mighty wave of conviction over his sinful soul did sweep.
He left the table. He had to find a place
Where he could pour out his heart for God's saving grace.

He did find a church, and ran to the altar that night
And again Jesus' blood washed a black heart white.
A dedicated prayer then reached the throne:
Father, Thy kingdom come, and in me let Your will be done.

Events then happened, he found his place.
In loving compassion he publishes God's saving grace.
He loves to preach his sermon on 'Why Pray'
Because it changed his life in such a wonderful way.

Bob tells a story of a man named Kim Gobb.
He too is an evangelist doing the works of God;
But he was so depressed, and feeling very bad:
'I think God has forgotten my number', to his wife, he said.

They were travelling. As the others ate, he went walking.
He passed a booth, a telephone was persistently ringing.
He took down the receiver and in a deep voice said 'hello'.
The answer he got caused his amazed mind to blow.

'Would that be Reverend Gobb?', the operator asked.
'As far as I know, its him', he surprisingly gasped.
'Operator, that is him! That's the voice I heard on T.V...
Do connect us up. I know he can help me.'

Mr. Gobb, its a miracle that at your office, I find you there.
Its a wonderful answer to a desperate prayer.
To commit suicide seemed the only thing I could do.
I'm in such a dilemma, I have no way through.

Sister, I'm 2000 miles from home, but I received your call
In a telephone booth. To hear my name, near gave me a fall.
'I was about to commit suicide, but to God I cried --
If You are there, please help me'. Something in me replied:

...And gave me this number to which I took note.
Could this be Kim Gobb's office? A lump came in my throat.
I decided to place a person to person call
And if you answered, it would be a miracle!

Kim led her to the Lord. What joy and rejoicing they shared.
He went back to tell his wife the surprising answer to prayer.
Dear wife, God didn't forget my number like I thought He had
Such a thrilling experience makes my heart leap, it's so glad

There are different levels in God's law of prayer:
Number one is 'Lord help me', the sinner's cry of despair.
But God wants us to develop, to mature and clearly know
What we are doing, and the fruit persistent prayer bestows.
98

Prayer is the greatest work in the whole universe,
Bringing eternal life to an eternal soul under an eternal curse
God cannot force His will on sinful rebelliousness,
Because of His love, through prayer, He gives forgiveness.

God will never work against His character of equity.
Neither will He do what He has ordained for you and me.
Praying selfish prayers, which fail the lost to Jesus to bring,
Will be unanswered, a waste of time, and not change a thing.

It is when a sinner repents, the angels in Heaven rejoice.
We must keep priorities straight, and fervently lift our voice.
We bind the devil's work -- release God's omnipotent power
To enshroud this world with Salvation in this closing hour.

Let us understand and hide it deep in our soul.
God ordained our prayer a superlative power to take control.
Its the prayer that will change things and make them right,
So fear not the mighty battle, but rejoice in the fight.

Faith Cometh
Romans 10: 17

Faith cometh. It cometh by hearing His Word.
The living Word in us, which is Jesus our Lord.
We can't work it up; or bring it down -- we have no way,
But the Word operating in us, will His faith display.
There is absolutely nothing that He cannot do.
All He needs is a clean emptied vessel to work through.
We must hear the Word, and it in Jesus Name apply;
And in all our situations, the power of the Word, not deny.
We have boldness and confidence by the faith of our Lord;
And love, unity, purity and power, according to His Word.

When we see that our flesh traits are sentenced to the cross,
God will give us the victory over flesh, sin and dross.
The last exhibition of Christ's Body shall top all the ages.
He'll produce His work through priests, prophets and sages.
A glorious victory He is about to manifest.
His work shall be finished and cut short in righteousness.
Then shall be the most wonderful reward
As we sweep through the gates with our victorious Lord.
To His Father He'll present His Bride, adorned beautifully,
And she shall love and adore Him throughout eternity.

99

A New Wine Skin

It takes a clean vessel for power that flows from the Throne.
Something so pure and so precious belongs to Him alone.
I must depend upon the Spirit to lead me into Father's will:
Flesh will break 'neath the pressure, and the anointing spill.
Yes. I want a new wine-skin Father, that is dedicated to You:
A clean, emptied vessel that You may work through.

I'm driven by a consuming desire to love and glorify Thee;
Transformed in Your likeness, so You are manifested in me.
Do baptize me Father, with Your holy, cleansing flame,
And accept my sacrifice in Jesus' atoning name.
Cause His attributes in this house of clay, to grow
Unto His maturity, to display Him wherever I go.

As I wait in Your presence, make Your way clear,
That I go forth with strong steps, void of all fear.
Open my understanding, Your wisdom and love fill my heart.
Keep me alert, that from Your purpose I shall not depart.
In this dark, dark world, make me a ball of flame,
Knowing the power of Your word and authority of Your name.

Here is my flesh Lord. I totally commit it to You,
That You can do Your own work, through me too.
Your work You'll finish in a quick, glorious way.
Jesus' virtue, glory and power we will spontaneously display.
Together we can do it because our eyes are fixed on Thee.
Through Your conquering name, we can have 100% victory!

Suddenly there will be a great shout from the sky,
And the Bride shall vanish, without a good-bye.
Those who love and long for their Bridegroom to come,
In a flash shall be caught away to enter her Lover's home.
She'll be presented to Father in great glory and grace.
No spot or wrinkle on her garments -- all He will erase.

His Bride hath made herself ready and calls her Bridegroom:
Great joy amid saints and angels. At last the hour has come.
Those not ready will be left. That will be a sad day!
Many will wonder why they too, were not caught away.
They missed their visitation: took no heed to their Groom.
He could no longer wait, so they're left to face awful doom.
Zephaniah 1:14-18: Matthew 9:17; Mark 2:22; Luke 5:38; Romans 9:28
100

O Wicked Heart

O wicked heart, why hast thou deceived me?
O wicked heart, you must be crucified.

The singer told a story, of how his wife went astray.
He loved and cherished her dearly, but still she went away.
She stood by her husband's side, and answered God's call,
Ministered faithfully for a season, then had a very bad fall.

Satan filled her heart with pride and mind with vain thinking,
And blinded her eyes to the sin in which her soul was sinking
He told her: 'You are a beautiful woman, fame is in your lap.
A glamorous career awaits you for which the world will clap.'

Leaving her heart broken husband, she chose her own way.
She enjoyed her sin for a season, delighting in fleshly display
But suddenly under a pile of metal she lay crushed and dead
The alluring career she had chosen, quickly ended, and fled.

A hill was her sudden death-trap because of falling, wet snow
Her husband was led by that way. Why, he didn't know.
Skid tracks told him of trouble: he must go quickly and see:
He found her beneath the wreckage, her time no longer to be

In his spirit he heard her give a dreadful, horrified yell.
He saw her plunge into gross darkness, an endless, fiery Hell
Some day she'll see what she missed and tear out her hair.
She forfeited the glory of Heaven for a ghastly pit of despair.

If we sow to the flesh, we will reap this awful reward.
If we sow to the spirit, a joyful eternity with our Lord.
Our race is about over, our die we have now cast.
Are we sowing to the flesh or spirit? Our Lord we will ask:

"Search me O God, and know my heart: Try me, and know
my thoughts, and see if there be any wicked way in me and
lead me in the way everlasting."   Psalm 139: 23, 24

"The heart is deceitful above all things, and desperately
wicked: Who can know it?"   Jeremiah 17: 9

"And I will give them a heart to know Me, that I am the Lord."
                                        Jeremiah 24: 7

101

My Prayer for Today

God's will is the final word in every situation.
We want it Lord, in action and occupation.
It is God Who determines what shall be done.
We want to be controlled by the Holy One.
Not a show of religious superiority to display;
But a loving compassion, just to walk in Your way.

We need not be crushed by needs or fleshly desire;
If Your Presence is with us, its all we require.
We shall be tempted to the depths of our soul.
Dear Heavenly Father please keep control.
That we be not sidetracked by what we feel or see;
But that our eyes shall be rivetted solely on Thee.

Love, confidence, peace and joy, sealed Your victory.
Now grant Your Body to mature in this reality.
We long for this transaction to take place,
And be filled with Your wisdom, knowledge and grace.
You said it Father, "Let the weak be strong"
And be fully persuaded, these promises to us belong.

You resisted the devil and put him on the move.
This authority You delegated to us, Your word to prove.
What You have endured for us is far beyond degree.
To Father will be presented a Bride, in beauty and purity.
This deadly battle in Your humanity You fought.
By the supreme suffering for us this victory was wrought.

We have nothing in the natural to enable us to stand,
Against the demonic forces under Satan's command.
But we can rejoice Satan is under our feet,
Over flesh, the world, and the devil, our victory is complete.
Its 100% victory, Brother Cerullo does declare:
Through the anointed word, which he does daily share.

Therefore we can demand Satan to leave us alone.
We are standing on what Jesus has already done.
The mighty arm of God is bearing witness,
He's bringing His Body forth in His righteousness.
As God's word is final in our every situation,
Demonic forces will give way in defeat and frustration.

Faith Without Struggle

"Jesus answered and said unto them, Verily I say unto you,
If ye have faith, and doubt not, ye shall not only do this
Which is done to the fig tree but also if ye shall say unto this
mountain, be thou removed, and be thou cast into the sea;
It shall be done. And all things, whatsoever ye shall ask in
prayer, believing, Ye shall receive."   Matthew 21: 21, 22

To move mountains and do exploits in God is what we desire
We've struggled and sought for that faith to acquire.
All of our natural efforts to make good fruit grow --
To the prayers we want answered, the Lord has to say 'No'.

I've tried hard to believe, but my mountain won't move.
Jesus wants me to see every good gift comes from above.
The faith I need is His faith -- a gift that He gives.
The better I know Him, the more in me that faith lives.

Regardless of situations, His faith stood the test.
He was steady, unmovable, and stayed steadfast.
All He is, to us He has given,
So He in us, could be our living.

His whole life was centred in the Father's will.
Not once did He His fleshly desires fulfil.
He had joy, peace, confidence and love;
Now He abides in us, His attributes to prove.

We can relax when we know He knows the way.
Whatever confronts us -- He is our ever present stay.
Don't let your heart faint, be terrified, tremble or fear
'For I am with you' are the words He wants us to hear.

His very life will through us flow.
His attributes will be manifested wherever we go.
For His mind and will, we are yielded and willing;
So His wonderful purpose in us, He's now fulfilling.

Believe it and you shall receive it.

My Prayer   Psalms 18:49

I want a healthy body to sacrifice to my Lord,
A cleansed container into which His Spirit can be poured;
A soul with Father's love to saturate,
A purified mind for the Spirit to operate.

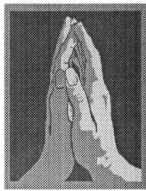

I want Jesus to be all my delight,
So He through me can do it right.
My youth is renewed, my steps ordained,
And my time is occupied in His name.

His word is my daily food,
With a loving relationship with my Lord.
I decree: soul, you must now repent
To fulfil the purpose which Jesus meant.

Forgive me and bring forth the fruitfulness I lack.
What the devil has taken shall be given back.
I want all you have ordained for me.
You're coming soon, so I don't want to be empty.

You're x-ray vision sees my heart, and You hear my cry.
You know the errors that I have passed by.
Through Your great grace, You paid for it all.
With confidence in Your almighty name, I call.

In the night You visit me and water my soul,
And give me that longing to be under Your control.
I need Your understanding and wisdom to see
The traps that the devil has laid for me.

Every avenue of my soul, I open to Thee
For the fulfilment of Your glory.
I love You and want to rejoice Your heart.
Grant the Holy Spirit to enable me to do my part.

Your praise and worship, may I not diminish.
I know what You start, You will also finish.
Oh Lord, attend to my prayer and hear my speech.
Build up the broken places, and repair the breach.
Your marvellous, loving kindness is sweet to me.
Make me the apple of Your eye, to glorify Thee for eternity.

Jesus the Healer of Wounds

A wounded spirit is such a devastating thing --
A train of evils it will surely bring.
The wicked pride gets dragged in the mud
And is chewed over and over like a cow chews her cud.

Hurts attract demons as honey does the bee
And the mind is plagued by them continually.
They don't give up until you are totally consumed;
The mind is bogged down and the spirit feels doomed.

There is a law to which we must take heed:
Hurts unattended is where the demons feed.
Don't let the sun go down on your grief.
Deal with it immediately and Jesus will give relief.

"Blessed is he whosoever is not offended in Me."
A fulfilment of My mercies in him there will be.
Satan, God's character and Word will malign.
He credits God with his evil all the time.

Satan is our constant accuser
Jesus is our faithful Intercessor.
The wicked accuser, with God's Word chase
And our faithful Intercessor lovingly embrace.

Our every need Jesus puts on the altar in Heaven,
Through His blood, pardon, healing and grace are given.
We must see pride, hurts and self pity, are dead on the cross
Resurrection life and power are freely given at a great cost.

If we nurse our ego's selfish carnality
We'll miss His presence and glorious reality.
Immediately attend to the hurts Satan will give
And in Jesus' healing, thrilling presence, joyfully live.

If we delight in the Lord and His Holy Word,
We'll put to flight the devil and his horde.
He can't stand our praising, worship and love.
Just enjoying Jesus puts him on the move.

God's Light and Word burns Satan like fire.
It tortures him and thwarts his evil desire.
All fleshly traits may we quickly recognize
So God's presence we can with joy realize.

Catering to the flesh only gives us grief
But delighting in Jesus is a precious release.
Our strength is in the joy of the Lord,
And will put to flight Satan and his horde.

He endured the cross, despising the shame.
We His Body, with His faith and anointing, can do the same.
We have the victory. It has already been bought.
Satan's power over us, Jesus brought to naught.

Our problem is not learning to live, its learning to die.
His resurrection life we do experience thereby.
Satan leaves a stink, and a grievous pain.
Jesus leaves a fragrance, crushing Satan's reign.

Real manhood, Adam sinned and gave away.
Jesus is the real Man, and His Body will display
His power, virtue, gentleness and love,
And be for His glory in word and move.

With faith in God's Word we can rip off the devil,
Defeat his onslaught and squelch his evil.
Let us be set like flint, with Jesus in the fray
And enjoy the victory our Captain will display.

Take the Limits off God !

"Cast Me not off when I am old, when My strength faileth"
                                    Psalms 21:9
"Let the weak say I am strong."   Joel 3:10

If I see God bigger than my weaknesses then I go forward.
If I think He can't do it then I go backward.
"But they harkened not, and went backward, not forward."
                                    II Chronicles 6:30
"I will multiply them and they shall not be few,
I will glorify them and they shall not be small."
                                    Jeremiah 30:19
Dear Father in Heaven, hallowed be Thy name.
Precious Holy Spirit your leading now I claim.
Let these longings in me burn with your fire;
To be a replica of You is all I desire.

My limitations are so many, I doubted You could do it.
But You are the mighty God, the all powerful Spirit.
You told me You would not give up till I was like You!
Such a glorious promise thrills me through and through!

I repent of wicked unbelief and spiritual iniquity.
Through Your blood I accept forgiveness, love and purity.
I'm so glad this transformation You can do;
And through the Holy Spirit, I'm brought into unity with you.

Let Father's love like a river flow,
To manifest You, Jesus, wherever I go.
Tune my ear to hear, and my heart to heed;
To relax in Your ability to strengthen and lead.

I want to thank You Lord with all of my heart;
In Your intercessory prayer line, make me a part.
With Your love and compassion, feel the world's great need.
Lets join the fighting angels, Your victory is decreed.

Touch this tongue with a coal from Your altar,
So I'll be Your sanctified, dedicated, undefiled daughter.
I'm so thrilled that it shall be; it shall certainly be!
This vessel of God's mercy is for Your pleasure and glory.

The God Who is More Than Enough
Habakkuk 2:14

I praise the Lord for this certain word,
Backed by the power and authority of God.
It stood every test and is so abundant,
All of Satan's tactics, it can supplant.
Bitterness and unforgiveness will wash away,
And wicked pride also cannot stay.
We must walk in forgiveness to be forgiven,
And be made a trophy fit for a holy Heaven.

It will take the washing only You can give.
Put that desire in us, for You to live;
To enjoy the joy You so abundantly supply,
And long for our meeting in the sky.
I love the encouraging words of Isaiah 52,
Of the end time works our Lord will do:
The weak made strong, the sick made whole,
And Your glorious power flooding our soul.

By Your name, on the serpent to tread.
Speak to the mountain: 'Go', like you said.
Not *say what we have*, but *have what we say;*
For a revelation of Your might in this day.
By Your judgments, they will learn righteousness.
In upset situations, have Your uprightness.
Your people shall fill the world with fruit
Even the devil will not be able to refute.

You will punish the world for its evil,
And look after that wicked old devil.
The earth shall be full of Your glory
And knowledge, as the waters cover the sea.
I'm aching for the fulfilment of this word,
And the world to see the ability of our Lord.
All appointed to wrath, hence they shall go
And all who want You, You they will know.

"That I might know Him, and the power of His resurrection,
and the fellowship of His sufferings, being made conformable
unto His death."   Philippians 3: 10

Kings and Priests unto God

A king is one in control
A priest is a minister for God to the soul.
This morning Psalm 21 gave me a thrill,
And my heart with His joy it did fill.

"Lord Jesus, I want that great rejoicing
To spring up in my soul like a fountain.
I'll be much stronger then I know
Because Your word tells me so. 1

Your great goodness makes me so happy inside.
Imagine: A crown of gold when I am Your Bride.
My youth shall be renewed 2
As Your blessings are bestowed.

I am waiting in expectancy. 3
My countenance is glad because of Thee. 4
I'm so happy because by You I am loved.
Through Your mercy I shall not be moved.

Jesus takes all our heartaches for us
When we in His word confidently trust. 5
Psalm 21: 9 tells me what You are after
I'll check it out in another chapter. 6, 7

You will destroy their fruit when You they face.
In Judgment, all sin You will erase. 8
None shall be able to stand before Thee
When You pour out Your wrath without mercy. 9

By Your strength we praise and sing
And rejoice -- You can do anything. 10
This anointed word, I "Amen and Amen".
Thank You precious Holy Spirit. We will do this again.

---

1. Nehemiah 8:10   2. Psalms 103:5   3. Proverbs 8:34
4. Proverbs 8:17-19 5. Ephesians 3:12   6. Ezekiel 21:5
7. Jeremiah 23:18-20 8. Zephaniah 1:18 9. Isaiah 10:3
10. Jeremiah 32:18

The Everlasting Blood Covenant

The Blood Covenant deeply touches my soul.
I long to understand, receive & enjoy its reality to the full
Through the blood every covenant promise comes into effect
Our lack of knowledge hinders these promises to perfect.

God's faithfulness and the power of the blood of Jesus
Has sealed this covenant to meet the needs of all of us.
It is as powerful today as when it came into existence;
Because He lived His life to God in 100% obedience.

This covenant of God with man is not just an agreement.
It is the closest and most sacred bond ever known:
All the riches of God, He made available for us to share.
They are already obtained for us, His word does declare.

He wants us to receive and rejoice in what He has done
Regardless of circumstances, our victory has been won.
All of Jesus, as the fullness of the Godhead, is in His Name.
He has given it to us that we through Him could do the same

In His Name is salvation, creativity, deliverance: all we need.
We call that Name and activate the promises He has decreed
We must see this Blood Covenant has fully equipped us
To accomplish His plan and purpose in this end time harvest

Thy people shall be willing in the day of power and holiness.
The day when His righteousness becomes our righteousness.
We must believe and live in the God of Miracles today
Or the circumstances and trials will turn us away.

A revelation of this truth will all fears dispel.
With eyes filled with Jesus and heart established, all is well.
'Go, I will be with thy mouth and teach thee what to say.'
Thus His work shall be finished in a glorified way.

'For He will finish the work, and cut it short in righteousness:
Because a short work will the Lord make upon the earth.'
Romans 9:28.

The Blood Covenant

What does the blood covenant mean to you?
Does our hearts appreciate what our Lord went through?
Do we realize what we can rightfully claim
Through the precious blood in that worthy Name?

It was in the garden He won the battle of the cross.
There Satan was defeated, regretting his loss.
He had to give up the keys to death and hell
When Jesus bruised Satan's head with His heel.

Can we see the door now open for us in heaven?
For every need we face, provision has been given.
There is no way Satan can jump our claim
Because Jesus signed all the cheques in blood and pain.

The blood ever speaks for us before the throne.
We can enter with assurance in its virtue alone.
On heaven's alter, Jesus places our needs there
And covers them all with intercessory prayer.

Amazing Grace

There is a desire that is burning in me
To do what I'm to do, and be what I'm to be.
I left this place discouraged and in pain;
I whispered Lord, I don't want to come here again.

I had a revelation of His divine grace.
Twenty years later, I'm back in this place.
A spiritual expectancy is growing in my soul.
I know whatever happens, God is in control.

I've peace, joy and confidence because I know --
His peace is sufficient wherever I go.
This revelation of grace gives me a thrill,
So I'll share with you to give you a 'Jesus refill'.

It was Father's presence that was manifested in His Son
Strengthening Him for the worst battle mortal ever won.
Jesus fully fulfilled Father's will, purpose and plan,
Then He passed that gracious anointing down to man.

That Heavenly presence is available for us today,
So we can fulfil His purpose in the very same way.
It's His powerful Spirit doing His works through man;
And His ending will be more glorious than when He began.

In those days, blind, unbelieving eyes were forced to see:
Common people doing the same as the Man of Galilee.
His courage, faith, and blessings possessed their soul.
Regardless of wicked retaliation, God was still in control.

We are now coming in on the last lap of God's finishing plan.
God is accomplishing His purpose through a yielded man.
He is doing a careful, personal work in the heart of each one,
Who long for His Kingdom to come, and His will to be done.

Now, let us take a look at this amazing great grace
And see in a world-wide way, what is taking place.
There is excitement, joy, faith, courage and zeal.
God working with them, confirming His work with His seal.

Satan is planning a very vicious retaliation,
To bring the saints into an impossible situation.
The spoiler will come, there's no way we can stand;
But the God of the impossible is holding our hand.

We will not be defeated, a great victory we'll manifest,
And God's finished work will be cut short in righteousness.
This is the day for our complete restoration,
Which the Bible calls the greatest visitation.

If we are not ready, it will be a woeful, sad story.
Whom will help you? Where will you leave your glory?
We now make our decision with whom we shall stand;
With the King of Kings or the Hell-bound Satanic band?

His empowering presence will enable me to be
The fulfilment of His purpose, He ordained for me.
He is no respecter of persons, He will do for each one
Whose reason for being is: Not My will by Thine be done.

There'll be joy, and rejoicing and satisfaction beyond degree,
As we sweep through the pearly gates to be His eternally.
The price of redemption shall be the Bride's holy praise.
This is Heaven's looked for, longed for, waited for days.

Remember, Grace is God's riches at Christ's expense.
He did it for us to save us from Hell's consequence.
Our life here is but a speck compared to eternity.
Let us consider the cost and make our choice wisely.

"You'll consider it in the end time"
Was Jeremiah's word from the Lord.

The Greatest Faith, Desire, And Fulfilment

The greatest faith is to believe God's Word.
Peace in all circumstances it will afford.
To speak His Word is a tree of life;
To be our strength and stay in this world of strife.

David knew, of God there would be a human manifestation.
The desire of the righteous would be a glorious realization;
So he prayed, I will be satisfied in that day
When I awake in Thy likeness in every way.

A longing to be like Jesus is the greatest desire,
An awareness of His presence we shall then acquire.
When His presence is with us we need not fret.
When He walked with His disciples, all their needs He met.

With Your loving presence please flood my soul
And with thankfulness I shall yield to Your control.
Just to be always there where You want me to be;
So Your fountain of living water can flow through me.

A thirsty sick world is crying, crying.
Needy, orphaned souls are dying, dying.
What am I here for, I must now know,
And what direction would You have me go?

In me let there be a cleansing deep within,
So in sweet communion I can walk and talk with Him,
And let the healing comforting Word freely flow
To bring help to the depressed wherever I go.

The greatest faith, desire, and rewarding commission
Is when we walk with our Lord in humble submission.
On Earth as in Heaven His will shall be done.
He will finish His work and a crown we will have won.

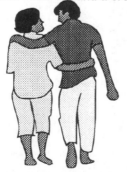

Just Leave it With Jesus

"Just leave it with Me" is my pillow.
He knows His will for each day.
He has the blueprint in Glory
And knows each step of the way.

Let's take all limits off Jesus,
Strike out our thought and will.
We cry for a clean wine skin, Jesus --
Always ready and available.

If prayer is needed at midnight
Or the early morning of day,
The Holy Spirit within us
Knows when and how to pray.

We must play the Man for our people
In all things, humbly seek His will.
We've been put here for a purpose.
Let Him that purpose fulfill.

If He breaks us in pieces -- Amen it.
Though we feel as small as a mite --
He'll make us then His tower,
Filled with Himself for the fight.

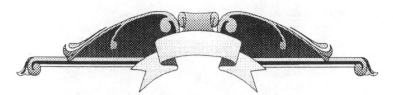

I Knew You'd Do It, Jesus

Last night I dreamed I felt the sweetness of the Spirit,
When I awakened I was saying, "Jesus, I knew You'd do it".
It is thrilling, waiting in expectancy.
To be one with Thee will be my ecstasy;

With Father's love flooding my soul,
And the precious Spirit taking control.
More precious by far than the wealth of the world,
Is the Abrahamic covenant with My wonderful Lord.

Grant a cleansing of this wine skin by Your blood
To make it ready for the avalanche of Your glory flood.
Purge my tongue. Make clean my mouth
For your gracious words to come forth.

Over this thirsty soul, waiting in expectancy.
I know it is coming, and it is coming to me.
May my steps be Your steps, Your ways mine too
So there'll be a quick finish of what You want to do.

In loving humility, just to walk with Thee,
And manifest Your presence in simplicity.
Your word tells me, this is what shall be.
I am delightfully waiting in expectancy.

I want Your wisdom, faith, and understanding
To do as You did, in serving and giving.
Let Your Kingdom come and Your will be done,
Because with You, You have made me one.

The Reward of the Righteous

There is the natural and there is the supernatural.
The laws of the natural are pain, death and burial.
The law of the supernatural in Christ, is life --
A restoration and victory over satanic strife.

Satan's aim is to turn us from the Lord
By causing so much pain, we can't receive His word,
Which we must receive in our present situation
Before He can give us His great restoration.

This means even in pain, we can have peace.
As we "Amen" His word, He gives release.
His light then, speedily shall shine
And restored health shall be thine.

As Acts 3:19 says, repentance precedes this blessing,
Then there shall come a great refreshing.
As when the body pains, something needs correction,
The pain of repentance is God telling us we need Salvation.

Many just say what they have in the Lord,
But we need to have what we say, according to His word.
The anointing will make us succeed.
He, through His word, can meet every need.

If we take His word into our heart,
It will change us and set us apart.
We will be to the praise of His glory;
His replica is Salvation's great story.

If we walk in God's word
It will keep us in the Lord.
Jesus is making a great finish of His purpose for man.
Before we were born, He had for us, a purpose and plan.

The reward of the righteous is beyond imagination.
He, in loving mercy will bring about our transformation.
He watches the fire that refines our gold,
To bring forth His likeness, and glory untold.

Epilogue to The Reward of the Righteous

Kenneth Copeland said: "Get into the word, and the word will get into you." These scriptures were upon my heart, when this poem came to me:

Romans 8:2 says, "For the law of the Spirit of life in Christ Jesus hath made me free from the law of sin and death."

2 Peter 1:4 says, "Whereby are given unto us exceeding great and precious promises: that by these ye be partakers of the divine nature, having escaped the corruption that is in the world through lust."

1 Thessalonians 2:13b) tells us, "The word of God effectually worketh also in you that believe."

Isaiah 58:8,9 says, "Then shall thy light break forth as the morning, and thy health shall spring forth speedily: ...the glory of the Lord shall be thy reward. Then shalt thou call and the Lord shall answer; thou shalt cry, and He shall say, Here I am: If thou take away from the midst of thee the yoke, the putting forth of the finger, and speaking vanity."

The word must be our reality: Jude v 24 "Now unto Him Who is able to keep you from falling, and to present you faultless before the presence of His glory with exceeding joy."

He can meet our need: Philippians 4:19, "But my God shall supply all your need, according to His riches in glory in Christ Jesus." John 17:19, "I sanctify Myself, that they might be sanctified through the truth."

Matthew 6:9,10 says, "Our Father which art in Heaven, hallowed be Thy name. Thy Kingdom come, Thy will be done, in earth as it is in Heaven."

Psalms 16:11 tells us His Kingdom is joy and peace: "Thou wilt show me the path of life: In Thy presence is fullness of joy: at Thy right hand, there are pleasures for evermore."

118

Solomon said in Proverbs 1:23, "Turn you at my reproof: behold, I will pour out My Spirit unto you, and I will make known My word unto you."

Acts 3:19 says, "Repent ye therefore, and be converted, that your sins may be blotted out, when the times of refreshing shall come from the presence of the Lord."

Ephesians 1:4,6: "He has chosen us in Him before the foundation of the world, that we should be holy, and without blame before Him in love", "To the praise of the glory of His grace, wherein He hath made us accepted in the Beloved."

Romans 9:28, "He will finish the work and cut it short in righteousness, and a short work will the Lord make."

Job 23:14, "He performeth the thing that is appointed for thee."

Daniel 12:10, "Many shall be purified, and made white, and tried; but the wicked shall do wickedly: and none of the wicked shall understand; but the wise shall understand."

Amos 5:6a, and 9:8 "Seek ye the Lord and ye shall live". "Behold, the eyes of the Lord God are upon the sinful kingdom, and I will destroy it from off the face of the earth".

Daniel 11:32b), 35: "The people that do know their God, shall be strong and do exploits... Some of them of understanding shall fall, to try them, and to purge, and to make them white, even to the time of the end."

John 9:31, "If any man be a worshipper of God, and doeth His will, him He heareth."

Zechariah 13:9 says, "I will bring the third part through the fire, and will refine them as silver is refined, and will try them as gold is tried: they shall call on My name, and I will hear them: I will say, It is My people: and they shall say, The Lord is my God."

Revelations 3:11, "Behold I come quickly".   119

The Shepherd and His Flock

God has given pastors responsibility and authority
Which must be guarded with honesty and integrity.
The responsibility of precious souls are under their care,
And the mysteries of the gospel, with anointing they share.
It is no small thing to be called, this office to fill,
But the Lord hath made provision to perform His own will.
Of wisdom and understanding, He hath laid up great store;
His Holy Spirit on His servants, He will outpour.

As we repent and in loving compassion pray,
God releases ministering angels to clear our way.
Just as He opened the eyes of Elisha's servant to see
The mountains filled with chariots for their delivery.
This kind of praying builds a wall to keep out
The wicked plots of Satan, which he is about;
But prayerlessness and judgement opens wide the gate
For Satan to come in and evil havoc manipulate.

We never should side with the wicked, lying press
And help slaughter one who has erred in unrighteousness.
If he truly repents, he need not carry a burden of guilt
For all the works of the flesh, the precious Blood was spilt.
Few realize the satanic assault against the ministry
That Satan has planned to mar for eternity.
We should minister in love to the one of ill repute
And reestablish him in Jesus, so he can bear much fruit.

Girls, glory, and the gold: Satan cashes in on these three.
Through them, he has brought down many a good ministry;
So pride, envy, jealousy, self-pity, egotism, and hatred let go.
Jesus forgives and pours out His Spirit. His word we'll know.
All that is fleshly shall go through His sieve;
Only that which is of Jesus shall be fruitful and live.
When we in unity and love hold up every Pastor's hand,
A mighty revival shall sweep over our land.

"Turn you at my reproof: behold, I will pour out My Spirit
unto you, I will make known My words unto you."
                                            Proverbs 1:23

120

Lord Send Your Fire   Romans 12:1

I want Your fire Father, I really do,
To consume all that is not of You.
Make this body an acceptable sacrifice,
Which is my reasonable service.

All that is carnal please consume,
Prepare me for Your Kingdom to come.
My limitations will not bother me
Because I know I'll be one with Thee.

Make my spirit a burning flame,
To fulfill the purpose You did ordain.
Let Your life like a river flow
To heal the hurts wherever I go.

Many loved ones are heavy on my heart,
Make them ready from earth to depart.
Your compassion to fill me is my goal,
To be Your extended hand to their soul.

Bring me into unity with Your Body,
And saturate with Your power and glory.
Its all mine through the blood You shed,
To give me power to walk on Satan's head.

Over my family, a defeated foe I see,
The whole package, in harmony with Thee.
I remit their sin, like You told me to do.
How You will do it, I'll leave up to You.

I'll praise You for the accomplished fact.
What the devil stole, he must give back.
I praise You for the answer to my prayer.
I long with each one, Your love to share.

With all Christian saints, I take my stand
For a sweeping revival to cover this land.
Grant a host to be ready to ascend,
When the trumpet blows and time will end.

Your Soul is up for Auction

Two mighty forces bid for your soul;
You make the decision who shall have control.
Your mind and will have this responsibility;
The decision to be made is for now and eternity.
We are born in sin and our hearts are full of evil;
So we feel more at home with the world, flesh and the devil.
There's no appreciation of the agony our Lord went through
To redeem our soul and a right spirit renew.

He paid the greatest price, our sin and iniquity to bear.
This blood bought possession, with Satan He shall not share.
To give up desires wrapped in fleshly lusts is a little to pay.
In view of eternity, what is the value of your eternal destiny?
Man was fully sold out to be the possession of the devil.
He has permeated all flesh to reap the punishment of evil.
Its a clear cut decision you must now make --
For Jesus or Satan: Which way shall you take?

Jesus' nail scared hands to you are outstretched,
Pleading His love and mercy, you will not reject.
He knows very well how horrible Hell will be.
His love for you is so great, He longs to set you free.
If it's too hard for you to leave paths of selfishness and sin,
It's because you have not experienced the new life within.
Old things pass away and all things become new --
He renews a right spirit and puts a new heart in you.

A new heart loves God and longs to do His will,
And all of His great mercies in it, He will fulfil.
He rewards you for what He can do through you --
He is your sanctifier, and your sufficiency to keep you true.
Blessed is the man that feareth the Lord
And delighteth greatly in His living Word. 1
All those that seek Him are loved and adored,
On all those who forsake Him, His wrath is outpoured. 2

---

1. Psalms 112:1   2. Ezra 8:22

If we perform the word of the Lord with all of our soul,
No need to worry about the world or devil getting control.
No evil tidings can make us afraid;
Trusting in Jesus, our heart is fixed and stayed. 1

We must be well girded with the two edged sword, 2
And firmly hold the shield of faith in our conquering Lord.
Wisdom, love, humility and obedience are the prerequisite;
They will gird us and guard us and make us fit.

This is the battle side of the picture, but wait and see --
The glories that await us with Jesus for eternity!
Don't hesitate to give up the glitter the devil offers to you-
Live whole heartily for Jesus, with eternity's values in view.

It's so thrilling when you give all of your life to Him
And be filled with His love to the very brim,
And be watching and ready when He comes in the sky --
To this wicked old world, shout a final good-bye!

---

1. Psalms 112:7   2. Hebrews 4:12

A Shaft in the Master's Hand

Lord make me a polished shaft in Your hand
To be shot forth at Your command.
Grant that oneness that makes a strong connection
So whatever is done, shall bear Your reflection;
And be totally delivered from flesh that domineers,
Being confident in faith and void of all fears.
To firmly stand in the will of my Father above;
Rooted and grounded in Your wonderful love.
Let Your loving compassion through me flow
To bring forth deliverance wherever I go
Just to be that shaft in my Master's hand
And regardless of what, to firmly stand.

Which Basket are You In?

In the sanctuary two baskets of figs appeared to me.
The Lord said, 'Jeremiah what do you see?'
Two baskets of figs, one is good, beautiful to behold,
The other is very evil and covered with mould.
The good figs are those who obey my word,
And go into captivity as I command, saith the Lord.
It is for their own good, I send them there.
I'll keep and protect them, and their life spare.

I'll plant and build them, and bring them again,
Into their land where they shall remain.
Even though they dwell in the land of the enemy,
I will protect and care for them tenderly.
I'll be their God and My people they will be
And with all of their heart they shall seek Me.
I'll reprove kings for their sake and make them a blessing
And stir up their spirit with joy and refreshing.

If they keep My word with Godly conviction
And hearken to the prophets' admonition
Myself in them I will glorify,
And their lives to Me they shall sanctify.
The bad figs are those who heed not My voice.
They do according to their preference -- their own choice.
    "The words that come out of our mouth, that we will do.
    We don't believe what Jeremiah said was true." 1

They shall find out whose words shall stand. 2
I have four enemies to sweep over their land. 3
The sword to slay, beasts to devour, and dogs to tear --
There will be no help or hope anywhere!
When I pour out my wrath, no hand can stay.
Because of their wicked rebellion, they all shall pass away.
Do we live our life by our preference, or our own intention,
Or a higher life governed by His word and Godly conviction.

---

1. Jeremiah 44:16,17   2. Jeremiah 44:28
3. Jeremiah 15:3

Mixing Carnality and Godliness is Deadly

"I'll cast thee out of My sight or spew thee out of My mouth"
Is His word to those who walk after the flesh, not the Lord.
The Lord praised Jehu for making a speedy riddance of
Ahab's family, then he walked not in God's way,
But his own way, which was iniquity.

Cursed is the one who on flesh does rely.
He will depart from the Lord, and His word deny.
The wicked heart fills with pride and doubt.
It strangles the faith that could bring them out.

From two tables we cannot eat:
The Heavenly mana, and Satan's spread of deceit.
We can't sneak things from Satan's table, and Jesus not see,
And we can't harbour evil thoughts, and the Spirit not grieve.

The Pharisee's were good people in their own eyes.
Their righteousness was filthy rags -- the Lord does despise.
With great pride, their hearts did swell.
Jesus said; 'Satan's children, who shall go to Hell.'

Jesus loves the sinner, and can set them free
But those who go their own way, walk in iniquity.
It takes complete submission and total surrender
For of His great restoration, to be a partaker.

"Be ye holy, as I am holy", Thus says the word.
It is time for the manifestation of the fullness of the Lord.
It is joy, pleasure, glory, and fun
Being one with Jesus, and seeing His work done.

An eternal reward beyond our imagination
Will be for all those who make this dedication,
But if from the flesh we just cannot part
The light we now have, shall become very dark.

"When your light becomes darkness, how great is that darkness."

A revelation of Jesus' love, and wonderful peace
Will dethrone old Adam, and Heavenly life release.
Glorified with His glory, and abandoned to His will,
Very quickly then, His purpose, He will fulfill.

The trumpet shall blow. We will hear the shout.
From this wicked world, we'll be raptured out.
We'll see Him, and like Him we shall be,
Presented to Father, the Bride of His love for eternity.

"Behold I come quickly, and My reward is with Me."
"The Bride says come."

The Conflict of Wills

I want to write a poem on the will as the key
That has opened the door to the world's misery.
The undisciplined will is like a wild bronco
That refuses to submit and be under control.
Three powerful wills rule this universe:
God, Satan, and man, whom he bound in his curse.
To retaliate, he ruined the man God made for His glory,
By beguiling Eve, he ushered in sin's ghastly story.

Each of these wills have a desire, purpose, and plan.
This deadly conflict is over the eternal soul of man.
Light verses darkness in this final fray:
This is the battle we're seeing today.
God made man with a will to decide
With whom he'd stand, and also abide.
A quality decision must be to stand for the Kingdom of light
Because we are born into a kingdom of the darkest of night.

Satan knows his time is short, his doom in Hell is sealed.
Millions he is taking with him, it is now being revealed.
The day of God's wrath on all sin; it too is manifest,
But whosoever receives salvation is rewarded and blessed.
The Bible tells us to consider our latter end --
So think, where will your soul eternity spend?
Jesus took all our sin and gives us His righteousness,
So with Him we'll share eternal, blissful happiness.
126

Carnality Verses Godly Reality

These words are coming to me today:
Precious Holy Spirit, teach me to pray.
There's nothing Father does not see;
Please Holy Spirit, search me, search me.
Two types of Christians we see are the carnal and the holy.
Our commitment to these determine our destiny for eternity.
My choice is Jesus, grant Your holiness be in me,
And all of my carnality be nailed to that tree.

Your Word says: If with all my heart I turn to Thee, 1
This veil shall go and Your Spirit shall give the victory.
Let Godly conviction now take control;
Show me the symptoms of a soulish soul.
Lord what does it mean, "The days of Ananias are here"?
These thoughts trouble me with an awesome fear.
Ananias and Sapphira claimed to do what they did not, 2
And they faked a blessing which they had not.

Many of My children see what I am doing;
Because of their carnality, pretend to have My anointing.
There'll be some drop dead because of this thing;
And an awesome fear of God, it shall surely bring.
Earnestly repent and cry unto Me
To recognize and reject the spirit of carnality.
You can laugh, but your heart shall still be sad;
You can act holy, but inside soulishness is bad.

Both of these Christians are now on display.
Those who are carnal and those who are holy.
The carnal judge the holy, for how they do and say,
Because they differ from their conventional way.
A manifestation is coming -- It is already here:
The difference to flesh walkers to those in Godly fear.
Lord give me a rest from my works. I'm sick of carnality.
I hate my flesh spotted garments. Make me like Thee.

---

1. 2 Cor. 3:16   2. Acts 5:3,9

The wrong in others I do not want to see
But deal, dear Lord, with the wrongs You see in me.
I long to be in this great restoration
To do Your work in holy demonstration.

Let Your loving compassion burn in my heart
For all of Your saints, of which I'm a part;
To be able to help them, there must be
This deep cleansing to take place in me.

The Holy Ghost is the only power in me
That can manifest Your word in my body.
It is a display for the world to see,
And they'll admit I've been with Thee.

Its not hard to know if I'm going the right way.
Just check the spirit I adhere to each day.
Is it according to my preference or Godly convictions,
I make my decisions and choose my directions.

I have been fasting and I have been praying.
This is what His Spirit to my spirit is saying.
I believe a like spirit is moving in you;
Let us pray one for the other, and to Christ be true.

From Which Cup Shall You Drink?

There are two cups of wine for us to take;
Of one or the other, we shall certainly partake.
New wine must be put in new bottles, saith He;   Mark 2:22
The old wineskins can't stand the new wine potency.
New skins are those saved, cleansed and delivered from sin.
This prepares them for the Holy Spirit to fill to the brim.

David said the Lord showed His people hard things
And the cup of the wine of astonishment it brings. Psalms 60:3
In the end time, judgment on His Church must fall.
A very great sifting shall come upon one and all.
A thorough cleansing of His people is now taking place
To prepare them to manifest His holiness, power and grace.

128

If we refuse to let go of all that is fleshly and sin,
There is no way that God will put His Holy anointing within.
A very strong spirit of preference domineers the soul, so
What we like, we do; and to what we don't like, we say 'no'.
Godly conviction does not work on this line.
You must do My will if you want My light to shine.
Daily we'll come to the throne of Grace
That the Lord's will and way in our life may take place.

If we sow to the flesh, we drink the wine of astonishment;
But sow to the Spirit and of His will, reap fulfilment.
We need wisdom, and the cross to make the flesh decrease,
Then the very life of Jesus, in us, He will release.
Thou hast given a banner to them that fear Thee   Psalms 60:4
To be displayed because of the Truth and reality.
We praise Thee for the power of Thy word,
And the inclusive provision of our faithful Lord.

What is Your Decision?

Come and be a part of the river of God
And learn how to be one with our Lord.
The wisdom we have, and talent display--
Can it sustain us in God's wrath today?
There is nothing in the world that we can do
To stop God's wrath, and His plan in view:
To end Satan with all his deceptive ways,
And make a new world for His glory and praise.
Right now a mighty battle is taking place:
Satan's power against God's power and grace;
Man is the battleground of this great fight.
We'll choose the wrong, or we'll choose the right.
Learn to be one with our victorious Lord;
To be hidden when His wrath is outpoured.
He'll quickly finish all He has said,
So choose life, or be numbered with the dead.
The reward for those who with Him stand true:
An exit from Earth to Heaven, with Him to rule.
If we suffer with Him, with Him we will reign,
And be delivered from Hell with Satan's domain.

Where Will You Spend Eternity

Who we choose as a model for our life role
Will decide the destiny of our eternal soul.
If the fear of the Lord is not our daily meat, 1
The fruit of the flesh, we shall surely eat. 2

The flesh has been corrupted since the fall,
So we dare not heed its lust and its call.
All our carnality must die on the cross,
Or inevitably result in eternal loss.

All of man's guilt, Jesus was willing to bear,
To deliver us from Hell and His life share.
Six times in Mark 9, our Lord does tell
The existence of an eternal fiery Hell.

Its utterly impossible that agony to quench,
And all Hell is permeated with a horrible stench.
There will be no water, not a breath of fresh air;
Not a wink of sleep, to ease the despair.

The 'Rock and Rollers' no more shall sing,
Their agonizing screams through Hell shall ring.
The backslider in regret shall tear his hair
When he knows he has missed Heaven for the pit of despair.

He didn't want to part with the world, the flesh and the devil,
So now he reaps their reward, the reward of all evil.
If we forsake the Lord for what we treasure,
We'll hate it for eternity and that without measure.

Hell is filled with hatred, cursing, and pain,
And eternal life, you'll never more attain.
The life we live here is but a drop in the sea
Compared to the expanse of eternity.
Do you think it is worth doing your own thing --
Sowing to the flesh and having a fling?

---

1. Proverbs 1:29   2. Proverbs 1:31

Dear Lord, I can't bear to see loved ones go there.
Please teach me to pray Your intercessory prayer,
To rescue them from this awful fate
And get anchored in You, Jesus, before its too late.

They work so hard, a living to make.
Its so easy for You and Your word to forsake.
If they could learn to take You in all they do,
You would bless their work and carry them through.

Lord, please do in me what must be done
To rescue lost souls ere my time is gone.
May a constant petition reach the mercy seat
To bring my loved ones into a victorious feat.

Shall We Choose Life or Death?

Simply receive, what He says He will do.
In every situation, He will bring you through;
So do not fear death, and do not fear life.
Jesus is the Almighty Conqueror over all strife.

Death is a sudden exit into the glories of Heaven
Exceeding the imagination at the rewards given.
To the very same degree are Hell's agonies:
Great hunger and intensified lust for iniquity.

No hope, no friends, a hellish decaying stench,
And a consuming thirst, no way to quench.
All you have to do, is let domineering flesh have control.
You'll land in the devil's Hell, an eternally lost soul.

Jesus died to close Hell, and open Heaven for us,
But it is our choice whom we will serve and trust.
We can choose His love and blessing beyond degree,
Or do our own thing, for terrorizing agony for eternity.

Peter said: "Pass the sojourn of your time here in fear,
Because your soul is destined for eternity.
You have been called to glory and virtue,
His promises make you a pattern of His nature."

Holiness Unto God

Holiness is not an option,
We must know its condition.
Its attributes are demanded -- essential.
And it is versus all that is carnal.

Because of it, no sin can enter Heaven.
It is within our reach, because it is God given.
We can't stand before it. It is so awesome.
The little I've experienced, I know I'm undone.

To bring forth fruits of holiness is the work of the Spirit
And is effective in us as we yield ourselves to it.
To the god of flesh, or of Holiness we give the control
To abide in and rule over our soul.

How do I know to whom I give this authority?
God's holiness is ever verses our carnality.
They are as different as darkness to light.
I come to the light automatically. It reveals my plight.

The self god is proud -- always gives others the blame.
It can't see its wrong but quickly can others condemn.
For example: the wrong in others I can clearly see,
But there is nothing much wrong with my good me.

The fear of the Lord is to hate all sin.
My own relationship with Christ is where I begin.
An inside longing makes me want to be like Him.
I don't even want my garments spotted with sin.

The words of my mouth make it very plain,
From which spirit they come and who has the reign.
Are they negative and hurtful like a sword of steel?
Or are they gracious words that comfort and heal?

That is why Proverbs is a book we should absorb.
It shows the way of Satan and the way of the Lord.
If I go Satan's way, his judgment I will receive.
If I listen to God, I'll inherit Heaven with those who believe.

132

God in His word has made it very plain,
How Hell I can avoid and Heaven gain.
What is my priority? Do I accept or reject
God's way of blessing, or an eternal hellish regret.

Jesus bore all of Hell's horrors to set us free.
It takes a quality decision to stand in that liberty.
He defeated Satan, solved the sin problem.
That work is done.
We must long for Jesus, and be for Jesus alone.

My Response is Vital

My response to God is so very important, you see
Because it opens the gate to His response to me.
My love and worship is the key
To bring me into the Spirit's harmony.

His great promises form in me His nature,
And will cause His likeness to mature.
If I lack this vision I'm blind and cannot see
What the blood bought covenant purchased for me.

My flesh will influence the choices I make
Which mould my character and my destiny shape.
What is my response, dear Lord to Thee?
Am I thrilled over what so soon shall be?

You paid a big price to set me free;
I don't want fleshly-will to manipulate me.
I want Your wisdom, knowledge and love
To follow Your blueprint in Heaven above.

When I read Your word, it gives me a thrill.
I know Your purpose in me You'll fulfill.
I rejoice in Your glory and feel Your joy too.
I shall be satisfied when I awake like You.

Does Jesus Expect Too Much of Us?

Why am I a sinner when I do all that I can?
I use my energy to help my fellow man.
I love my family, ministering to them day and night.
Their problems are mine, and for them I fight.

To my work there is never an end --
Why do you put on me an extra demand?
Is God blind? Can't He see my present load?
Is this the God you say is your wonderful Lord?

I certainly appreciate the situation you are in.
That is not why I emphasize the destiny of sin.
We are all born in sin and shaped in iniquity,
Children of Satan, he wants to dam for eternity.

We can be adopted by our heavenly Father
Through the sacrifice of His Son, our elder Brother.
He thereby closed Hell's door and opened Heaven for us,
If we'd accept His pardon and in Him put our trust.

There are laws to adoption, to which we must give place --
To be accepted in the Beloved is a product of His grace.
When we open wide our heart and invite Him in
We dedicate our life, and our occupation to Him.

He'll work all things to our good according to His word.
If we believe, Heaven's great riches on us shall be poured.
Satan's main aim is to keep us from glorifying the Lord
Bringing discouragement and trouble to turn us against God.

If he can convince us, the best we can do is the way,
He's accomplished his goal, and sealed our destiny. 1
No way can the carnal life be converted and saved --
Reckon it dead to receive the resurrection life Jesus gave.

He gave Himself that He might redeem from all iniquity;
And have a people who long for His life and purity;
To be a sacrifice well pleasing to God Who shall supply
All your needs according to His riches in glory. 2
134

He wants you to see God as bigger than your circumstance.
His great grace is sufficient for the needed endurance.
So receive and believe. What He says He will do.
If there's no way at all, He'll make one for you.

For His great love and peace, we've nothing to compare;
If we willingly suffer for Him, His great glory we'll share.
You have been called to glory and virtue.
His promises make you a partaker of His nature.

The reward for being willing, His cross to bear
Is the glories of Heaven, to which nothing can compare.
It is God Who worketh in you to do His good pleasure.
Submit to His working, receive His love without measure.

The seed of the first Adam is corruptible.
The seed of the second Adam is incorruptible. 3
All that is corruptible, to Hell is destined.
The incorruptible goes to Heaven with the redeemed.

Peter said: 'Pass the sojourn of your time, here in fear.
Because your soul is destined for eternity.'
The fruit of our decision is passed to our descendants
And will be sorrow and grief, or life abundant.

---

1. Jeremiah 17:5   2. Philippians 4:19   3. 1 Peter 1:23

Does Jesus Make Mistakes?

Does Jesus make mistakes? The Bible says: No.
He alone knows our heart and why we choose our way to go.
We are born in sin and love the flesh ways we are in.
They are tainted by Satan when he plants his nature within.
We are born in sin; we will walk in his way.
His demons watch over it to increase it each day.

Our path is stormy we get wounded and sick.
Satan's plan of retaliation is without reason and quick.
Now we are in a mess with no way out.
People turn against us, our selfish ego will pout.
We eye people who seem to have all they need.
A demon slips in called Covetousness and Greed.   135

The dear Lord sees our sad situation.
In loving mercy, reveals His great salvation.
His gracious light illuminates our darkness.
Our spirit has a new life in His righteousness.
But our soul has a process it must go through.
Our will decides here, what we shall do.

Our undisciplined spirit also enters the play
To make our will decide rightly, is a daily fray.
Now if I let my flesh life reign,
I frustrate God's grace and Christ's suffering for me is vain.
My will must sentence my flesh god to the cross, Galations 2:21
Or I'll produce Satan's likeness and be lost.

How to fight this battle, His promises He has given.
To cope with carnality in the natural -- no way under Heaven.
Jesus said, I'll purify your dross and remove your tin.
He's the finisher of His business, we must leave it with Him.
This purifying process, He calls a fire.
He tempers it to bring forth the gold He does require.

We find ourselves in situations we do not like.
Often end up with Christians with whom we'd like to fight.
What I am, they are not. What they are, I am not.
Flesh rubs flesh and friction forth is brought.
Out of my mouth goes a sarcastic word;
As Solomon says, like a sharp edged sword.

Was this God's idea, to be with one the like I was not?
Not in appreciation and love, but to my shame, I fought.
Because of my flesh, I was hard on them too.
Jesus undertook. We loved when we were through.
Little by little, my dear Lord let me see --
The wrong I saw in others, was the wrong He saw in me.

He healed my hurts, gave me a longing to be like Him
And see my flesh through His eyes and hate its deadly sin.
I'll soon be 82. Many fires I have been through.
Greatest trials became greatest joys if I took His cue.
I love His correction and I love His rod.
He is preparing me to be like my God.
136

I must not limit God by my limitations
But see my circumstances are for my transformation.
If I rejoice in the trials and the testings,
He'll bring me forth for His glory in great blessings.

Two Types of Wisdom

Today two types of wisdom flood the world:
One is from Satan, and one is from the Lord.
The word shows their source so we can clearly tell
The destiny of one is Heaven but the other is Hell.

James three, verses thirteen to eighteen
Lets their difference be clearly seen:
If our goal is for Heaven's applause,
Then our life will not be a lost cause.

For Godly wisdom, there will have to be
A cleansing and release from carnality.
The words we say determine our destiny;
To be serpent minded, the serpent has the sway.
                                    Matthew 12:34
Satan before man, shall cause deceit to prosper,
And roll out the carpet for Antichrist to enter.
He will adorn Satan's wickedness very beautifully,
And the world will be fooled by his deceptive ability.
                                    Daniel 9:12
Antichrist shall come forth as an angel of light,
And by a miraculous power, make the wrong look right.
Two great forces hinder the progress of this man:
Christ's Body and the Jew, whom he'll kill if he can.

The whole world shall run to receive his mark --
Dead sure that he will give light instead of dark.
He will solicit their love and their loyalty
To wipe out his enemies with Satan's cruelty.

A sudden shocker shall then take place:
Those filled with Godly wisdom and grace,
Shall vanish and be with their victorious Lord;
Then God's great wrath on all shall be poured.

Salvation -- The Right Choice

You are like three people who live in one house:
The spirit, soul, and body live together in us.
When God created this wonderful capacity,
They were full of wisdom, love and purity.

Satan beguiled Eve. In disobedience, she sold out to him.
Adam, though he knew better, also partook of her sin,
Then Satan entered into the man God created for His glory.
Thus we have written the world's sinful story.

Satan knew he was sentenced to Hell.
To get back at God, he trapped Eve and she fell.
God in His great mercy pitied condemned man
And thought up a wonderful salvation plan.

His progressive plan unfolds from Genesis to Revelation.
We see how God has brought about a great restoration.
At His appointed time, He took our place and died for all sin.
It only works for those who repent and faithfully serve Him.

He created man with a will to decide
The one he chose to serve for eternity with him would abide.
The race is about over. The end is in sight.
God's evaluation is coming. Have we chosen right?

God's Spirit is calling you. He does not want you to go
To Hell where untold agonies for eternity you'd know.
His love for you is so great He is able to transform you
Into a trophy of grace and His will you will want to do.

Its such a worthwhile living. Why get messed up with sin?
He'll bring you out of darkness into marvellous Light within.
Oh the love and peace when He makes our sinful heart white,
Then you can look up to Jesus and say: "I have chosen right."

The Last Hour

Before the world was, Jesus was there.
He and Father planned the hour he had to bear.
Jesus would have to be slain:
God's wrath on all sin on Him was lain.
Father knew it would be a ghastly hour,
But Jesus' unconquerable Spirit had the power.
It was a perfect plan for man's redemption
And manifested God's love intervention.

He needed a new creation to end Satan's behaviour.
The creation of man was brought into the picture.
To fellowship with God and enjoy the garden was real life.
To Adam had been given a beautiful wife.
Adam and Eve were counselled not to eat of a certain tree.
If they did, they would experience death immediately.
Satan watched to get Eve alone, the easier to deceive.
He set his trap. She fell for it and him she believed.
Adam knew better, but from his wife that fruit received.

Then all of Adam's authority, Satan had.
From the garden they had to go. The situation was bad.
God has great love and compassion for man --
Right then His great plan of redemption began.
God will have a righteous world again
In which restored mankind with Him shall reign.
He Who knew no sin would be made sin for us.
And we full of sin, would be made His righteousness.

Jesus had to empty Himself of all God's glory
To become our scape-goat bearing our sin and iniquity.
Jesus relinquished His life to do His Father's will.
We must do the same, His purpose to fulfill.
Our will is the key to our restoration.
We must be submissive to His decision.
It may have taken 5,000 years for this hour to come.
All things were ready -- His great work He had done.
Then was a great preparation with Father, in prayer.
He well knew the agony He would have to bear.

His disciples could not understand the grief of His Spirit.
When He tried to tell them, their inner ear couldn't hear it.
John 17 was an all inclusive prayer for this hour:
His Church and Himself needed God's glory and power.
We with the Father and Son, were then made one --
The greatest battle ever fought, in this garden was won.
Ministering angels strengthened Him. His hour had come.
He and His disciples went to meet Satan's army alone.

Jesus in control: "Whom seek ye?", He shouted fearlessly.
'Jesus of Nazareth.' He strongly declared, "I am He".
By the Spirit of His words, all backward fell immediately.
"Whom seek ye?" 'Jesus of Nazareth', they said fearfully.
"I told you, I am He. If you want Me, let these go their way."
This too was the Voice of authority, they had to obey.

Peter cut off a soldier's ear. "No Peter, put the sword up.
This is Father's will. I must drink the dregs of this cup."
Jesus healed the ear and to the head priest said: Hither to
When I was daily in the temple, nothing you could do.
This is your hour of darkness and power, I give Myself to you
Like a criminal, they took Him to the judgment hall,
The Lamb of God and glorious Conqueror of them all.
To Annas, son-in-law of the high priest who had prophesied:
'It was necessary for the people that one Man should die.'

To Caiphas. John knew him and his heart was terrified.
He got Peter who was so scared, 3 times the Lord he denied.
A cock crowed. Jesus passed by with a love look in His eye.
Peter went out full of grief and remorse, and wept bitterly.
They took Jesus different places. Finally to Pilate's hall.
Pilate's wife said: 'Have nothing to do with that Man at all'.
Pilate's attempts to deliver were curtailed by the angry mob.
He knew He was innocent and feared He was the Son of God,
But he sent Him to be whipped, striped, bent over the post
And tied. He was sentenced to receive thirty-nine stripes
By the cat of nine tails with metal tips.
A big soldier stood ready to administer it.
Jesus' legs drew up in agony. His flesh and blood did fly.
Each one of those stripes, our healing did supply.

They put on a purple robe and crushed thorns into His head,
Plucked out His beard, spit on Him, slapped and mocked;
His body bled. Pilate said: 'Behold the Man, a King.
I find no fault in Him.' The screaming mob wanted Barabbas.
If you let Him go, you're not Caesar's friend.'
So Barabbas was released and Jesus was condemned.
Pilate could not forget the Lamb without spot or blemish.
Because of the horror of it all, his own life he finished.
They put upon Christ's torn body, a hundred pound cross.
His eyes blinded with blood, He fell. His strength at a loss.
A Roman soldier kicked Him with his heavy boot;
A group of women, cried and lamented over such a brute.
"My daughters, weep not for Me, but for yourselves cry.
If they do this in a Green Tree, what will they do to a dry?"

Simon followed carrying His cross up Calvary's hill.
Here Jesus would complete the last scene of Father's will.
They nailed Him. "My Father, forgive them", He prayed.
God's love so much stronger than Satan's hatred, displayed.
Then in a hole, that heavy cross was dropped.
Every torture and pain, in His body was wrought,
But a perfect Salvation our precious Lord bought.
He looked at His mother, and committed her to John,
Who lovingly cared for her from that time on.

One crucified said, 'Lord in Your Kingdom, remember me.'
Jesus said, 'You will be with me in Paradise today.
The blood I am shedding will wash your sins away.'
The joy of that, strengthened our Lord's endurance.
Three hours of darkness swept over that terrain;
Holy Place curtain 4" thick, top to bottom, ripped in twain.
The ninth hour, Father could not look on sin, turned away.
A loud cry: 'My God, My God, why hast Thou forsaken Me?'
They gave Him vinegar to drink. They could go no farther.
Another loud cry: 'It is finished'. He was committed to Father
A Roman soldier pierced His side with His sword.
Out of the wound flowed blood and water, which showed
He died of a broken heart, carrying the world's sin load.
Satan had suffered utter defeat and loss. In His weakest
Unaided state Jesus conquered: God's Lamb upon the cross.

141

The Beachhead of the Devil

I cannot fight an enemy that I do not see.
The real beachhead of the devil is in my 'me'.
There are two worlds in which we live;
To one or the other, our life we give.
There is the natural and spiritual realm:
We make the choice whom we place at our helm
Two mighty forces continually seek the control
Of our sin cursed nature, which is our mind and soul.

The flesh is condemned -- it's full of sin and iniquity.
It can't please God. It is against Him in constant enmity.
According to the flesh, we judge, live, walk and move;
But death is the finishing line of our fleshly groove.
We think our flesh is good and wise; but its filled with pride
That builds a strong wall, our wicked ego to hide.
We are prisoners to our carnality,
To which the second death holds no reality.

It is not possible for fleshly eyes to see
The evil spirit forces that works through the 'me'.
But Jesus came, and condemned sinful flesh and set us free
From this bondage of corruption, into His glorious liberty.
His wonderful Spirit, to us He did give
To mortify the deeds of the flesh, and live.
Now there's a battle raging deep within:
Who is going to rule? Who is going to win?

It's our decision. We choose who shall have control
And who shall sit on the citadel of our soul.
I must be ever watching and alert to see
How the enemy through the flesh, tries to manipulate me.
"No weapon that is formed against thee shall prosper; and
every tongue that shall rise against thee in judgement,
thou shalt condemn. This is the heritage of the servants of
the Lord, and their righteousness is of Me saith the Lord."
Isaiah 54:17

Hezekiah's Revival

In the Bible we are told of a mighty battle fought.
God sent His angel and a great victory wrought.
Ahaz' rule brought Israel into big trouble with God,
But Hezekiah's mother prepared him for the chastening rod.

God's cup of wrath was full and ready to spill.
This hero of faith determined to make it nil.
Ahaz put lights out, broke vessels, locked the temple door.
He plunged Israel deeper into sin than she ever was before.

Isaiah was Hezekiah's right hand man;
Together they prayed and God gave them a plan.
The priests were told that they were God's chosen to stand
For Him in performing His ministry for fallen man.

With all of their heart they must repent and seek the Lord
So they could stand in the gap and defer the wrath of God.
They sincerely repented and covenanted to do God's will.
To cleanse the temple was the King's mandate to fulfil.

A thorough cleansing and sanctification then took place.
Lights lit, alter repaired, broken vessels were replaced.
Early, Hezekiah called priests and rulers to the house of God.
They brought their sin sacrifices to be offered to the Lord.

As they repented and made their dedication
Hands were laid on the offerings for their reconciliation.
The priests now ready, stood in their place for action.
Now the rulers prepared themselves for God's transaction.

The Levites sang, the trumpets were blown.
Since Kings David and Solomon, such rejoicing not known.
The Israelis joined the King in worship and praising,
And God stirred up their spirits with great rejoicing.

Hezekiah sent letters from Beersheba to Dan
Telling them to come: This is God's move, not man.
The priests renewed their dedication
To be prepared for God's visitation.

So they came with their sacrifices for their sin.
It was too much for the priests, so the Levites stepped in.
Other priests who had not made their consecration
Could not take their place and fulfil their commission.
Hezekiah prayed for them and they were restored,
And got in their place and worshipped the Lord.
All brought in their tithes in abundance
Which to God is a very sweet fragrance.

The priests from twenty years old and upward, in humility
Were in their place and preformed their duty.
Hezekiah with all his heart sought God and on Him relied.
God honoured and protected him on every side.
Sennacherib, King of Assyria, with a very great host
Determined to kill Hezekiah at any cost.
Men speaking their language harassed their king
To make them too fearful to fight, and an easy victory bring.

'Hezekiah is deceiving you, you could never stand
Against our mighty forces with your little band.
The God you serve cannot handle us;
We are the conquerors, in whom you'd better trust.'
Hezekiah comforted his people: Fear not, God fights for us.
With God we are stronger than they. Praise Him and trust."
God sent an angel who killed Sennacherib's mighty men.
He, shame-faced returned home to be killed by his own kin.

This is a picture of what is going on today.
We will see God's wrath in an unprecedented way.
The Body of Christ is standing in His wisdom,
Jesus supplies health, peace, joy, power, and Protection.
This will be God's ending of the earth and the human race.
We must rise up and take our God-given place.
We are in big, big trouble. Israel is too.
There'll be one relationship that is noble and true.
It's been prophesied, a holocaust on Israel shall break
Two-thirds of their number it shall suddenly take.
The most massive destruction shall be brought forth.
God's people shall stand glorified to be His mouth
To speak His word, which is stronger than all Hell's forces,
Which shall prevail against all Satan's tactics and curses.

144

Canada and the States shall also be overcome.
God's broom of destruction sweeps sin that has overrun.
God is the Finisher, dear saints take heart.
He is our faithful Protector and Supplier in the darkest dark.

Suddenly the spoiler shall come to ruin us in every way.
We must with the whole heart seek God, wait, and pray.
An avalanche from Glory of holiness and power
Will fill His clean new wine-skins in this closing hour.
God never sends judgement before He sends His grace.
Now with joy and rejoicing we must stand in our place.

Joel 1:14   Zephaniah 1:17-18, 2:3   Daniel 11:32
2 Chronicles 29:30-32   Isaiah 10:3, 11:4, 11-13
Romans 9:28   Zechariah 12:3, 8-10

A Weapon of God's Warfare

Much about horses, God's word does tell:
They were good fighters and went till they fell.
In Revelation, two white horses we see --
But they are different as different can be:

Revelation 6:2 is the Antichrist from Satan; he is earthy.
19:11-16 is Jesus; from the omnipotent God -- heavenly.
The Antichrist has a bow but there is no arrow to win.
He's wickedly cruel. Satan controls him from within.

A crown is given him and he is allowed control until
The God of Heaven accomplishes in him His will.
The great dragon is no match for the Yahweh Jehovah God.
He is gathering the nations for his wrath to be outpoured.

The great day of God's wrath, none shall be able to stand:
With His broom of destruction, He is cleansing our land.
Sin is so sticky. If you hold it, you will go out with it,
And forever be in Satan's company in his hellish pit.

God is ushering in a new world of righteousness and glory --
The climax of His justice and salvation's gracious story.

145

Jesus: Teacher, mighty Conqueror, Protector, Deliverer

I am the Lord thy God which teacheth thee to profit,
which leadeth thee by the way thou shouldest go. 1

Put on the Lord Jesus Christ and make no provision
for the flesh to fulfill the lusts thereof. 2

Put off the old man which is corrupt according
To the deceitful lusts. 3

I will make you My goodly horse in battle. 4
They shall tread down their enemies
And they shall fight, for the Lord is with them. 5

The Lord of Hosts shall defend them in that day. 6
Thou shalt still the enemy and the avenger. 7

Destroy Thou them. Let them fall by their own counsels.
Cast them out in the multitude of their transgressions;
for they have rebelled against Thee. 8

But let all those that put their trust in Thee rejoice:
Let them ever shout for joy, for Thou defendest them:
Let them also that love Thy name be joyful in Thee. 9

With gladness and rejoicing shall they be brought forth. 10
None of them that put their trust in Thee will be desolate. 11
Not by might nor by power. By My Spirit saith the Lord. 12

Curses, the way of death -- the dead horse.

They hearkened not and went backward and not forward. 13

But the Lord is the true God, He is the living God,
and an everlasting King; at His wrath the earth will tremble,
and the nations will not be able to abide His indignation. 14

Oh daughter of My people, gird thee with sackcloth
for the spoiler shall suddenly come upon us. 15

146

That day there will be great shaking in the land of Israel. 16
The riders on horses shall be confounded. 17
Woe to her that is polluted. She obeyed not the Voice;
She received not correction; she trusted not in the Lord;
She drew not near to her God. 18
The wicked are turned into Hell. 19

I saw the dead stand before God and the books were opened:
And another book was opened, which is the Book of Life,
And the dead were judged out of those things which were
Written in the books, according to their works, and
Whosoever was not found written in the Book of Life
Was cast into the lake of fire. 20

---

1. Isaiah 48 : 17;   2. Romans 13 : 14;   3. Ephesians 4 : 22;
4. Zechariah 10 : 3; 5. Zechariah 10 : 5; 6. Zechariah 9 : 16;
7. Psalms 8 : 2;   8. Psalms 5 : 10 b; 9. Psalms 5 : 11;
10. Psalms 45 : 15; 11. Psalms 34 : 22; 12. Zechariah 4 : 6;
13.Jeremiah 7 : 24; 14.Jeremiah 10 : 10; 15.Jeremiah 6: 26
16. Ezekial 38 : 19; 17. Zechariah 10 : 5; 18. Zeph. 3: 1, 2
19. Psalms 9 : 17;   20. Revelation 20 : 12, 15

I asked the Lord, what does it mean, "I will make you my
goodly horse in battle?" And He said, "A horse does not
know how to fight, but he has been trained to be one with his
rider. He knows what the touches mean, and knows exactly
what his rider wants him to do."

"You are My horse, and I am your Rider."

This horse is the happy winner
because he is one with Jesus,
the Almighty Conqueror.

This poor horse, panicked and died.
He carried the wrong rider.

147

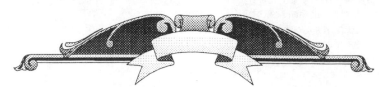

His Goodly Horse in Battle

I've been adopted into Abraham's line,
The great promises God gave him, are also mine.
I can be His good horse in the battle today.
His almighty Spirit in me knows the way.

The Conqueror is my Rider, so I need not fear.
His word, love, grace, and mercy are my gear.
David said: "My people shall be willing in that day",
Jesus, in great agony: "That they would be one", did pray.

In the natural, the horse does not know how to fight,
But it is trained to be one with the rider for the right.
A quick glorious finish, our Lord will make,
Then all His good horses from earth, He will take.

His broom of destruction, shall sweep every place;
And woe to all those who have rejected His grace.
The spoiler shall use every tactic in his book.
To defeat this army, God from his ranks took.

The Bride goes up triumphant without a sin stain.
A glorious reward He'll give her. With Him she'll reign.
If we repent of our sin and open wide our heart,
With Jesus in this battle, we can all do our part.

There is a White Horse Coming

I see a white horse galloping. His Rider wears a crown.
He is the Mighty Conqueror, the foe He will put down.
He is leading an army arrayed in dazzling white;
A replica of the Leader, and one in the fight.

The weapon they are using is the Word of the Lord;
Wielding it in faith by the Spirit's sword.
There is nothing that can stand before them.
The devil has to flee.
Jesus is leading His army in a mighty victory.

They are the saints who bought His gold tried in the fire,
And come through trials and testing, gaining their Desire.
Now they have attained to the highest place --
The trophy presented to Father through His amazing grace.

Enliven Your Word -- write it on our heart.
Let Your mind be our mind, and Your compassion impart.
Fill our hearts with Your fear, knowledge and grace,
So we won't miss out on this last great race.

All we want is to do Your will.
Your life in us; this desire will fulfil.
It is Your will and You can do it too.
Our aim is just to glorify You.

All the works You did, do now in us.
A great harvest of souls is our trust.
You healed the sick, the bound set free, and raised the dead.
Everywhere You went, the Gospel of the Kingdom was spread

In that army, we now are a part,
But search us, Dear Lord to the depths of the heart.
Dislodge any carnality our eyes fail to see;
Fill with rejoicing and make us jubilantly free.

The Horse and His Rider

I am the horse and He is my Rider.
On all decisions, He's the Decider.
He knows what is best for me, you see.
When I leave it with Him, I'm happy.

I wanted to balk and go my own way.
I lost the fight and the victory.
Suddenly then, my Rider was gone --
I was frantically defeated from then on.

I wept and cried, 'Come back to me'.
'I'll be your good horse obediently.'
Back came my Rider. He heard my cry.
With Him on my back, I know I'll not die.

He knows exactly what Satan's about.
With His word, He'll put him to route.
I cannot fear when the battle gets hot.
With trust in Jesus, the victory I've got.

Author's Note:

I was writing the second verse of this poem and
the Spirit told me to write it in the first person.
I knew there was a reason but didn't know what.
Early the next morning, it came to my spirit:
I'll explain your poem to you. I was happy that
the Lord was going to explain my poem to myself.
'Verse 1 was when you obeyed me and went to China.
You trusted me to meet your need. I was with you
in all your experiences there. When you had no way,
I made one for you. I brought you safely back home.
Verse 2 was in Hearst and you married out of My will
and you were in big trouble. You deeply repented
and cried unto Me. In verse 3, I came to you in hard
places. Verse 4 is your restoration. This year I will
come to you greatly, because you will need Me greatly.'

Mabel Black at seventy-two years of age, in Parksville B.C.

Horseback Riding

A long time ago, when I was seventy-two.
I decided to go horseback riding, which I loved to do.
I didn't know that horseback riding was an art --
If done correctly, you were with your horse, a part.
I have been unloaded because I did not do it right,
But I loved horses, and riding them was a delight.
However this time, I took a bad kink in my back.
I couldn't let my horse run since my back felt cracked.
I patted his neck and told him we would have to poke.
The line behind me did not think that was a joke.
They wanted to go fast. They knew how it was done.
If they had my back pain, it would not be so much fun.
I showed my chiropractor the snap that caused the pain.
It is funny now, but I will not go horseback riding again.

They Learned to Pray

See the world with friends who know the way:
The secret of their success -- they learned the way to pray.
The God of creation in them is doing great things.
Throughout the world awesome worship, and praise rings.

We can do it. We can do it. This is our day.
Holy Spirit is our Helper and Teacher. He knows the way.
He's the Almighty God of love, mercy and grace,
Empowering each member to finish a victorious race.

His divine purpose and plan we're seeing Him fulfil.
His Body is preaching His Kingdom, and doing His will.
His glorified army now manifested shall be.
His glory is flooding the Earth as waters cover the sea.

A restoration of years that the canker worm has eaten,
Is now taking place, and Satan is being beaten.
There is a world wide explosion of powerful prayer;
In deep repentance, full surrender, His Word they declare.

Satan's retaliation is raging in every place,
But the saints are overcoming by Jesus' grace.
Light is stronger than darkness, darkness has to flee.
Jesus is leading His Church in a glorious victory.

Multitudes turn to Jesus through the strategy of prayer.
Jesus' marching prayer teams go places; no church is there.
They claim that territory in the name of the Lord,
Then the Lord's love and deliverance on them is poured.

Multitude thousands are being gathered in
From violence, satanic corruption and sin.
This explosion of prayer ministry is sweeping the universe.
Desperate people are crying for deliverance from the curse.

Not only the holy but the hungry -- God hears their cry.
Hope, joy, comfort, and deliverance is His reply.
The Holy Spirit tells them where to go and what to do;
Whether they live or die, with Jesus they boldly go through.
152

Don't be side tracked from this great prayer call.
In this final restoration, we must yield to Him our all.
Even if the enemy force is thousands, and we are but one;
With Christ in the battle of battles, our victory is won.

God in judgment is laying the battle, accomplishing His plan.
It requires a quality decision and putting off the old man.
No flesh can glory in this great move God is giving.
We must put on Christ and let Him be our living.

What is a Prayer Warrior

The Battle Zone of Prayer was preached by Larry Lea.
I praise the Lord for the impact it has had on me.
I'm sure our precious brother will not mind
If by the help of the Lord, I get these facts to rhyme.
Now turn to Daniel 10 which is his launching base
And see Daniel, a mighty praying hero of divine grace.
In a not too distant time we shall stand before Jesus, to hear
And receive His evaluation of our earthly career.

We will be happy and rejoicing, as we hear His loving word:
'Thou faithful servant, enter now into the joy of thy Lord.'
Or before His presence in great shame, regret and fear
We'll hear: 'Depart into utter darkness. Don't come here.'
In the Bible are many promises for the overcomer:
'I will grant you to sit with Me and eat the wedding supper;
A new name never used before shall I give unto you;
Great is your reward as in great trials you stood true.'

Those who shun the path of the cross with its shame
Shall be cast into darkness in remorse and pain.
Whether we be overcome, or be the overcomers, that day
Will be determined by the way we learned to pray.
Are we going to be a prayer warrior? Are we going to pray
Or are we too busy? Listen to what Brother Larry has to say:
'The church is in the greatest conflict the world has seen.
The situations shall worsen, the like has never been.'

Satan knows his time is short and is nearly gone.
He also knows Larry and his warriors will not run.
They have set themselves like flint, their eyes on the goal.
God's fighting angels over Satan's host have control.
Our army shall go to cities; the gates of Hell we'll kick in.
Not an inch will we give up. In Jesus' name, we win.
We are going forth in Jesus' Spirit.
No doubt in my mind -- we are going to do it.

To the devil and all doubters, Larry declares today:
'This prayer army business is here to stay.
I stand with my God in a covenant, and I heard Him say:
No man, or demon of Hell can stand in your way.'
The gainsayers hate this way. To them it is sin,
But with the Lord we have covenanted. We shall surely win.
Daniel is our pattern and gives us a prayer fighting profile,
And against all of Persia's mighty demons he did prevail.

There are territorial spirits under satanic authority
To dictate over the natural world and enforce his policy.
Because Daniel in fasting and great intercession did pray,
God could send forth his angels. Satanic forces gave way.
The world we live in shall never change
Until the prayer army is in place and range.
There will be no harvest until we learn the way to pray;
The principalities and powers of darkness will be held at bay.

Thus the will of God can be instituted in the life of man.
Blindness and darkness shall flee in God's perfect plan.
Just to say revival is coming is a dream in the land of nod.
A revival shall not come until the church does her job.
'Pray ye therefore', then shall the great harvest come in
Light and glory shall replace blindness and sin.
When we do spiritual warfare, we push back the evil force;
Then the will of God can be instilled and have free course.

This massive harvest cannot come unless we do His will.
Each member of His body must this mandate fulfil.
The prayer warriors shall overcome demon forces and fears.
The non warriors shall be destroyed in the next few years.

154

God did not call us to a life of ease, void of trouble and pain.
'Rejoice in the fire. Be of good cheer. All of this I overcame.'
There is glory, joy and strength when we sing in the fire.
This is God's plan for our victory which we must acquire.
Our joy and rejoicing, we cannot procrastinate
Until the battle is won -- then it will be too late.
This pleases the devil, and he shouts with glee:
When we fail to rejoice in the fire, we lose the victory.

Until you learn to sing in the fire, in the fire you will stay.
Rejoice and Jesus brings you out, strengthened for the fray.
A prayer warrior must follow the pattern Jesus taught.
This kind of prayer brings Satan's strategies to naught.
Jesus knows the most effective way to pray.
This is the answer He gave His disciples that day...
There are seven distinct parts in this pattern, we see,
That cover the seven great needs of our life effectively.

We pray each part with open heart to God in communion.
Our inner man becomes strong in the oneness of this union.
Without a healthy relationship with God as our Father,
For the battles we are facing, we shall have no power.
If we don't walk in forgiveness, we will be in frustration.
If we don't receive forgiveness, we'll walk in condemnation.
If we forgive not others their trespasses, and iniquity,
Our bitter backbiting will expose us to demonic activity.

We must make a daily commitment praying every line;
Ever seeking forgiveness and forgiving others all the time.
If we sit in angry bitterness, planning to retaliate,
Death is working in us -- if this is the way we take.
Every day we must unclog the arteries of the man within,
Then shall we hear from God and walk and talk with Him.
From the very heart of God, we receive this vision:
For every need of our life, this prayer has been given.

Be a prayer warrior, not a prayer worrier --
Allowing the trials of life, our mind to commandeer.
In doubt, we offend God, by the negative things we say,
A prayer warrior in faith declares 'You have a will and a way.'

I put my foot down declaring: 'Thy kingdom come.'
In my life, marriage and children, 'let Your will be done.'
No demon of Hell can stand against Jesus my Lord;
And all that He is, for us, He has outpoured.
Every one of us should get involved in this army and be
In the place He puts us, standing against our enemy.
On the horizon, I see a cloud the size of a man's hand --
I know its the army of God defeating Satan's band.

Lock our spirit in solemn agreement for city and nation;
Identify with this prayer ministry to bring forth His fruition;
Activating His fighting angels in this worldwide warfare;
Establishing His kingdom, doing His will by faithful prayer.
Every day our heart is set for God, unclogging our arteries
Of fear and doubt. Be in place with prayer warrior families
To pull down the strongholds of Satan in our world.
God is leading that army with their victory flag unfurled.

God shed His blood for this great harvest of the world.
If we give ourselves to His cause, we will not be deferred.
'Our Father Who art in Heaven. Hallowed be Thy name.
Thy Kingdom come. Thy will be done in Earth as in Heaven.'
Lord I thank you for giving us Larry Lee.
This wonderful teaching, please work out in me.
Along with it, please add Your backbone, grit and grace.
My limitations, with Yourself replace. I thank you, Father.

The Blessings of a Prayer Warrior

What makes God's children not ready for His coming?
Love of money, complaining, and doing too much talking.
We'll be ready if we whole heartedly become an intercessor,
Being intimate with the Father, Holy Spirit, and Saviour.
To accomplish this relationship,Holy Spirit will teach us how
There's no time to procrastinate, listen and act now.
Do not do all the talking. Learn to hear what God is saying.
In so doing, we will obtain total satisfaction in our praying.
If we confess our sins, His word we'll know, 1
And His wisdom, and revelation through us will flow.
He has many rich blessings ready for those who pray,
We need to enlist in His prayer army today.
156

Our prayers will be answered. We'll enjoy His divine health.
Though economy fails, Father has stored up for us, wealth.
He will illuminate His word, and of His joy, we shall partake,
And the Holy Spirit will guide and protect, each step we take.
David saw our day as the day of holiness and power,
Also a willingness in God's children for this hour.
There is a conflict between Satan and God's power and glory.
God is making a clean up on sin's wicked, sad story.
There is an explosion of prayer in a worldwide way.
Romans 9:28 says He'll finish quickly, so we can't delay.
Lay aside every weight, and humbly our sins confess.
Put off the old man. Be clothed with Jesus' righteousness.

Many at this time will be confused and fall
Because they heeded not the Lord's last call.
Great, rich blessings are for those who will pray,
And wait expecting to hear what the Spirit will say. 2
We dare not in our strength, attempt to fight the foe,
Wait for His clear leading, where and when to go.
We must submit to, and rely on Jesus for this hour,
And He'll pour out His Spirit of love, joy and power.
According to our need, will be His abundant grace,
Whether it is life or death, we be called to face.
The prophets earnestly desired to live at this time,
Of complete restoration for which we must get in line.

Dividing walls shall fall, and unity forth, shall spring.
God's Kingdom established, and He shall be King.
Brooks will dry up. People won't know the way.
The arm of flesh shall fail, Jeremiah 17:5 does say
Larry Lee says: 'Four things God wants us to carefully note:
In God's plan and purpose, His Spirit is bringing about.
We must see ourselves as the head and not the tail,
And we can fulfil His purpose, and not fail.
We must live within our means, debt is a curse,
Which He bore in Galatians 3:13, that curse to reverse.
Our tithing and giving done with cheerfulness,
Then He'll open His great fountain of blessedness.'

---

1. Proverbs 1: 23   2. Proverbs 8:34

Am I a Soldier?

The life of a soldier is very comparative
To the life God is calling His children to live.
The day on which the new soldier signs in,
Is the day a drastic change in him will begin.

To break the self will, is the first fray.
All of his worldly crutches are taken away.
To learn obedience is a rigid, hard role.
A mighty revolution must take place in his soul.

Under strict discipline he learns to do what they say.
His own desires and feelings are all swept away.
Through very great suffering, he combats the foe.
His whole life now, is under army control.

Man's army uses cruelty, harassment and pain
To forge their soldier and implicit obedience obtain.
The Lord has a very different way to accomplish this goal,
First He forgives our sins, then His love makes us whole.

God longs for a people to serve Him with delight,
A people whose love to obey is foremost in life.
A renewed mind, under the Spirit's control,
Will work God's will into the depths of the soul.

The desire to do His will, their motive underlies,
And it truly becomes the driving force of their lives.
They, like Jesus, can look up to the Father and say,
I'm not here to do my thing, but to walk in Your way.

In John 17, a picture of this sweet fellowship we see.
Verse 23 -- 'Father love them, even as Thou hast loved Me.'
Daniel said the wicked will be more so and evil will increase.
Joel said a mighty wave of anointing, the Lord will release.

James 5:7 will take place without a doubt.
Those who are ready, the Lord will take out.
His wonderful Spirit on us, He'll outpour ...
His glorious prize is well worth going for.

158

A seventy-seven year old, broken-hipped lady, I hear you say,
'Could never be a soldier in that helpless way.'
I agree that my body is, temporarily, out of commission
But my spirit is strong, and to His leading, I'm open.

I was talking to the Lord on the 'make me better quick' line.
He said: No, you're there for a purpose. You'll get out in time
'I guess I'm doing alright, and I'm really quite happy inside,
So, if that's Your will, Lord, it's O.K. with me', I replied.

There are some things in the future, I'd love to do,
But only if they are according to You.
I am happy to lie here while my broken bones, You mend.
I know I'm still your soldier and that You are my Friend!

A Mother in Trouble   Psalms 102: 1

I was in a battle with no strength to fight.
My brain was confused, which way was right.
A chorus in the Spirit, then turned the tide.
I didn't feel Jesus, but He was there by my side.

On the inside of me this chorus was sung,
And a soothing, healing then begun.
My fainting spirit, it did console.
And revived my downcast, sinking soul.

I will ride, I will ride, on the wings of the storm.
How to do this I've longed so to know.
Then the Spirit whispered, so sweet to my soul:
With your conquering Saviour, you go.

Some day you'll thank Me for the troubles you're in.
'Really Lord?! Then right now I'll begin.'
I threw up my arms, and praised my wonderful Lord:
And His sweet Spirit, on my parched soul was poured.

The clouds are His chariot He rides upon,
And He walks on the wings, on the wings of the storm.
He makes His angels ministering spirits, for our availability,
His ministers, a flaming fire, to perform His word perfectly.

I am hungry and thirsty and I want to be blessed,
And by the Father's Spirit of power, be fully possessed.
I need a daily supply of Jesus' life giving flow,
To give drink to the thirsty wherever I go.

God has planned no defeats for me,
His faith, courage, and endurance is also free;
But the flesh bars must be broken so it can flow,
And fruits will spring up and grow, grow, grow.

If I prove not my Lord in circumstantial tests,
How can I believe for outstretched hands to be blessed?
I want to be a joint worker for my Lord.
He poured Himself out for me, so let me be outpoured.

It may look like defeat by some demonic thing,
But on the scene comes Jesus, my conquering King.
I'm not in the battle alone, He is by my side;
Under the shadow of the Almighty I abide.

Jesus feared not the enemy. He knew God's Word is true.
In the hottest battle, He passes His authority on to you.
So take all limits off of God, stand on His Word and see
His omnipotent power will work for you and give the victory.

"No weapon that is formed against you shall prosper."
                              Isaiah 54:17
"I will restore health unto you, and heal all your wounds."
                              Jeremiah 30:17

A Song of Victory

I am a devil chaser. I'm not chased by the devil.
Christ suffered and died to deliver me from his evil.
I do not stand in my limitations.
The Holy Spirit in me is my sanctification.

From all evil forces, He will not run.
He's the Almighty God enforcing the victory won.
The devil hates me being in this place,
Learning to use God-given authority and stand in His grace.

The devil is using every evil trick
To wear me down, and make me sick.
I'll go to my teachers -- they know how to pray,
And send this sleep robber on his way.

I will speak to this mountain. It will have to go.
Matthew 21:21 declares that this is so.
I'm learning in confidence to use God's word,
And to put Satan to flight, his hopes deferred.

I know this battle is too strong for me,
But Jesus put me here with His guarantee.
I'm a member of His Body, which shall be
Brought forth in power, grace, glory, and purity.

To do God's will as Jesus did, we need His anointing.
Live it, enjoy it, and the Spirit will do the manifesting.
The purpose in testing, I have been told,
Is to burn off the tarnish, and purify the gold.

Active Faith

We need this faith, these dangerous days
To change our lives and destinies.
If we boldly confess, then we will possess. 1
With Satan, emphatically disagree, 2
But with Jesus, fully agree. 3
Jesus doesn't think like me: 4
I want to see to believe, 5
But He says: "No, believe and see." 6
Mark 11: 23 gives us the key: 7
Speak to your mountain, and it will flee. 8
'Nothing shall be impossible to you.' 9
Faith, God's word does believe;
Doubt, God's word does not receive. 10
We must speak God's word without fear,
And loud enough for Satan to hear. 11
This exceeds our circumstances and feelings by far,
When we call things which are not, as though they are.
Meditate on these things day and night. 12
They bring us out of darkness into light. 13
We'll hear the trumpet and vanish out of sight. 14

1. Mark 11:23,24   2. John 17:14
3. John 17:21,22   4. Jeremiah 32: 38-40
5. Isaiah 55:8   6. 1 Corinthians 12:31
7. John 21:29   8. James 4:7
9. Matthew 17:20   10. James 1:7,8
11. Romans 4:17   12. 1 Timothy 4:15
13. Acts 26:28
14. 1 Thessalonians 4:17

Unity

The hardest hour for Jesus had come
And a desperate prayer poured forth to the throne:
Father, glorify Me for this crucial hour.
I have manifested to them, all Your names and power.
This great plan of salvation now rests on Me
To purchase man's redemption and set them free.
I have manifested to them all Thou art
And how they, with Thee, through Me, are a part.
Father knit them together in our precious union
That in loving oneness, they will enjoy our communion.
Father, also may My joy in them fulfil
And as I have done, so let them do Your will.

Let all believers in oneness be
As Thou, Father art in Me, and I in Thee.
Then the world shall see this glorious manifestation,
When unity and love are displayed in holy demonstration.
In Hell the devil also had a plan
To keep them separated with their eyes on man;
But what Jesus declared surely shall be --
Something wonderful is happening right now we see.
Ministers are coming together to pray.
Lord knit us in love and have Your own way.
Something tremendous is about to take place --
A world wide restoration of God's saving grace.

The demons are frantically trying God's saints to kill;
To keep them from fulfilling God's perfect will.
There is an army arising who firmly shall stand
In loving compassion gripping each other's hand.
What a glorious company we shall behold.
They have come through hot fire and come forth pure gold.
A glorified masterpiece, they shall be,
Lovingly adoring their Bridegroom throughout eternity.
Now don't you want to be a part
Of these so precious to our dear Lord's heart;
And in intercessory prayer with every saint stand true.
There is a special place in this group for you.

The Walls are Coming Down

Denominational walls coming down is something to see.
From every church, people are coming to Thee.
They are sick of the dryness and worldly shine.
They have tasted something that they call new wine.
Jesus said old wineskins can't abide the new wine potency,
But new skins can handle it effectively.
That means religion is not open to the Sprit's move,
Because it is stuck in a man made groove.
David said 'Because they regard not the work of the Lord
They too shall be destroyed'.
They don't understand, Satan has clouded their mind.
To the mighty works that God is doing, they are blind.

Every move of the Spirit has been like waves in the tide --
They rush in so far, stand still, then backslide.
This great wave coming is going clear through,
And will finish the work the Church has failed to do.
Don't get caught in the great undertow.
It will suck you into darkness where many shall go.
Just keep riding the crest of the wave,
With your eyes on Jesus, the mighty to save.
They will love one another, desiring to be one.
As is in heaven, so in them shall His will be done.
The world will be wide eyed when they see
How the Lord has answered His prayer so effectively.

His arm is made bare in a world wide way.
The exploits of His Body are now on display.
Satan is trying all God's saints to kill,
He is defeated, the great plan they will fulfil.
These trials just serve to purify the Bride
And teach her in the Branch to abide.
As she draws from Him every breath of Life,
She'll overcome Satan and all his strife.
If you read your Bible, you will see
God is performing His Word very quickly.
We must decide now where we stand --
With the mighty Conqueror or the defeated satanic band.

Come Lord Jesus

Revelation 22: 17

"And the Spirit and the Bride say 'Come';
And let him that heareth, say 'Come';
And let him that is athirst come;
And whosoever will, let him take of the water of life freely."

Gird Thy sword upon Thy thigh, Thou most mighty,
And in Thy majesty and power, ride prosperously.
In Your truth, meekness and righteousness
Bring forth Your Body, in Your likeness.

Your beauty in them is what You desire.
Your faith in operation, is what we require;
So pour out Your Spirit -- our mouths are opened wide,
Power to be Your Counterpart, and purity to be Your Bride.

Adorned in garments of needlework so fine
With great joy and rejoicing, in the love which is Thine.
A cry to our Lover, 'Come quickly. Do come!'.
We long to be with You when our work here is done.

The answer, from the throne, is so precious and sweet:
`I'm coming, My beloved, when our work is complete.
My undefiled virgins, My blood you've applied;
To God you'll be presented as the Lamb's spotless Bride.'

So don't be afraid. I'm leading the way.
I'm longing too, for this looked-for day.
You'll be adorned with God's glory and be crystal clear --
Be greatly encouraged, the crowning day will soon be here.

Heaven's Armoury is Opened
Ephesians 6: 10 - 19

A heart repentant in humility
Will fear a state of carnality.
His precious blood that sets us free
Will clothe us from His armoury.
His mind is the helmet of protection,
Against the target of Satan's onslaught;
For if he can conquer our thinking,
The control of the soul he has got.

The Spirit takes God's righteousness
And the breastplate He works in us.
With safety and peace He will bless,
And with the Holy Word give rest.
His word gives us His authority,
Girding our loins for the fight.
Our hand holds the sword of the Spirit
To bring down the wrong for the right.

The shield of faith He gives us
Will stop every fiery dart.
Demons are persistently trying
To fatally wound every heart.
Our feet, He's shod with the gospel
To give the sick world His peace.
From the horrors of Satan's bondage
To enjoy His gracious release.

In the Spirit's anointing keep praying.
It will give needed strength to stand
In the place for us He has chosen --
An extension of His almighty hand.
The doors will open to greet us,
His voice so sweetly shall flow;
And with the anointing within,
The harvest will quickly come in.

Lord Jesus help me to don Your armour today --
To be clothed with You Jesus, and Your life display;
Able to withstand every dart of the devil.
In Your enduring faith, face the trials and tests of evil.
In Your righteousness, speaking the truth to set people free,
And declaring to the devil: "We have 100% victory!"

Father, Spirit, and Son are united with me. We are one.
In this covenant with Him, His will shall be done.
To enter this spiritual union with Him, means to be mature,
Fully equipped, perfected, to the measure of His stature.
In faith, love and unity, we agree
That this indwelling Christ shall manifested be.

Walking with Jesus

Its such fun just walking with Jesus
With God's love flowing through us.
It doesn't take any one special
For the Almighty Spirit to fill.

Such joy being one with Jesus,
We don't worry what we will do;
For He has the blueprint in Heaven,
He'll bring us triumphantly through.

All praise to the Father in Heaven
Who came up with so great a plan.
It took all the sufferings of Jesus,
The wide gulf of man's sins to span.

And prepare the way for the Spirit
To sanctify His counterpart Bride,
Presented to Father, on her He'll gaze --
His masterpiece fills Heaven with praise.

Beyond the Concept of Man
God is Performing His Plan

We need not run but face the storm,
In God's presence it will transform.
Watch Jesus change curses into blessings,
And be cleansed and purified in the testings.
"The weak shall be strong", Zechariah did say,
"David's fighting spirit they shall display."
In Daniel's prayer pattern we can pray,
And Persia's force will have to give way.

In Elijah's chariot, ride the wings of the storm,
This is God's finishing day, His word He shall perform.
In the spirit of Elisha we can enter in.
In God's end-time plan His Church shall win.
We will be filled with the Spirit like dear brother Philip,
And in the courage of Peter, rise up and do it.
And in the love of John, we can firmly stand
And be united in Spirit like Gideon's band.

In the meekness of Moses, manifest God's graces.
In the skills of Nehemiah, build the waste places,
And fulfil Paul's vision of Christ's Body triumphant;
And find our place in God's army militant!
Today in God's overcomers, these patriarchs we see,
And there is a place here for you and me.
The keys to enter are repentance and giving,
And in full surrender to God, Who is our living.

Such joy and rejoicing shall flood our souls.
We can laugh at the devil -- God is in control.
We can sing in the fire like the three Hebrew children,
And demonstrate loyal love like David and Jonathan.
I'm aching to get in on this battle, even though I'm eighty.
With Him I can bloom and bear fruit for His glory.
You can too! Just open to Jesus, all of your heart.
When we are yoked with our Lord, we can all do our part.

The Fast that God has Chosen   Isaiah 58: 6-14

Loose the bonds of wickedness; let the oppressed go free;
Undo the heavy burdens and feed the hungry;
Clothe the naked and do not seek to hide
From your own flesh which must be crucified.

Then your light will flash on quickly,
And your health spring forth speedily.
The glory of the Lord shall be your reward,
And His righteousness in your heart poured.

Prayer quickly answered, His blessing releasing;
Warfare prayer throughout the world is exploding.
It is fasting, repenting and a desperate cry
That opens the glory gate to the divine supply.

An undisciplined spirit hides deep in the soul --
It hates fasting and being brought under control.
It is filled with Satan; it is his launching base
To keep us from maturing in God's saving grace.

We must throttle all of our carnality
To have a clean heart for this reality.
When our words are His words, Satan will flee
And then we will experience the end-time victory.

It takes a clean, holy body for this sacrifice.
Are we willing to submit and pay such a price?
Willing to exchange our fleshly heart
For the Lord's nature to impart.

Sin is so ghastly in the eyes of a holy God.
Without repentance, we'll pass beneath His rod.
We dare not let a thing hinder God's last call.
Right now we must decide, and yield Him our all.

Don't point the finger and speak vanity,
And your darkness will be as the noon day.
A repairer of the breach you shall be.
A restorer of paths for others to see.

Only a willing heart can pay this price,
And have a body qualified for sacrifice.
Such joy and rejoicing, and glory to be had.
Regardless of the price, we'll be so glad.

Don't seek your pleasure or delight.
Love and serve God with all your might.
You'll ride the high places, declares His word;
And feed on God's heritage. Thus saith the Lord.

I want to adhere to these things, and pray.
Now who will go with me, this anointed way?
There will be no regrets for what we may go through.
When we see what Jesus has prepared for those that do.

He Meets My Every Need

He is the Healer of my body,
He is the Blesser of my soul,
He is the Fire in my spirit,
And I am under His control.

I give to Him, and He gives to me,
This blessing He has decreed.
I love Him, and He loves me,
And He meets my every need.

Play the Man for Your People

To be the man I want you to be
You must yield your life entirely to Me.
Know that My Word is reality.
No sin can stand My equity.

My blood can cleanse and set free.
As Father sent Me, so send I thee.
As I yielded to Father, His will to do;
Likewise He'll fulfill His purpose in you.

An abundant entrance shall be given thee.
I've prayed for our oneness, and it shall be.
Fear not the commitment I asked you to make.
But your part in My army, confidently take.

Life and death are in the words you say,
So let My gracious words flow unceasingly.
Love all My Body with a pure heart,
Prayerfully desire My grace to impart.

You judge from the hearing ear and seeing eye.
I judge the motives -- I hear the heart cry.
Leave the judgment to Me. I make no mistake.
All dross and tin from each one, I can take.

171

Holy Spirit be My King

O Kingship of the Holy Spirit, bear the rule,
In the paths of holiness, let me be schooled.
You learned obedience through Your suffering --
Therefore I dare not bypass this training.

Self-pity hinders God's purpose:
Reliance on flesh is a curse. 1
If we do not get what God want's us to receive
Around our mountain we'll go, until we believe.

This is the time God is speeding up progress,
Replacing our carnality with His righteousness.
'In that day, My people shall be willing'. 2
A quick work then, shall be the fulfilling. 3

There is a division now taking place,
From those who want God at any price
And those who refuse the sacrifice,
Replacing it with self-righteousness.

Teach me to stop Satan's cruelty
And defeat him in his evil villainy.
I can do it. That's why Jesus came --
To give me the authority in His name.

Waging war against those suicide bombers,
Reversing the curse, Israel to deliver.
In this great prayer army, please fit me in
To bring forth Your glory amongst all of this sin.

She greatly pained, but the victory won.
The woman travailed and brought forth the Son. 4

1.Jeremiah 17:5   2.Psalms 10:3
3.Romans 9:28   4.Revelation 12:5

Two Fires Coming Our Way

Two great fires are coming our way.
Its time to repent, fast and pray.
A might battle is raging in the heavenlies:
Jesus faces Satan in the battle of eternity.

Satan now has man where he wants him to be,
And he through man is sinking the world in iniquity.
By adultery and fornication he's corrupted society
With rape, bloodshed and abortion cruelty.

Of this sin God shall bring a speedy end.
Those involved in it, into Hell shall descend.
Diseases never heard of before are taking their toll.
Those indulging in this lust, damn their soul.

A Pastor, for a lost world was praying;
For deceived Christians, he was interceding.
Panic seized him, "My God what does this mean?"
He was taken from his body and saw a frightful scene.

A fiery star three miles across to earth was heading.
'Lord, don't let that fall in the sea, his soul was pleading.
Revelation 8:8 "A fiery mountain is cast into the sea"
Then millions would be plunged into eternity.

Satan is enlarging Hell in wicked glee.
He has ruined the man God made for His glory.
Through the cares of life, many have turned away,
And are deaf to God's way of life for today.

Scientists are watching that star in fear.
They say it looks like the end is very near.
Their computer needle points to disaster,
And the world is being torn apart by war.

The world is crying to Satan to bring in his christ
To stop the war and make everything nice.
Satan will oblige them; he already has his man,
And will slip him into power as soon as he can.

173

Jesus also has a surprise for Satan. He too has a plan
To be demonstrated through restored fallen man.
By a cleansing fire, a baptism of love and power they'll bring
A harvest of souls, they'll snatch from under Satan's wing.

Jesus learned obedience through suffering. We do too.
Even in cruelest of pain, God's grace takes us through.
As Jesus did, they do the same,
And pray for their enemies in Jesus name.

According to God's word, this is His greatest visit to man.
The thrilling part is we can all fit into His plan.
Limitations mean nothing because it is by His Spirit.
Just do as the Spirit says, the God in us will do it.

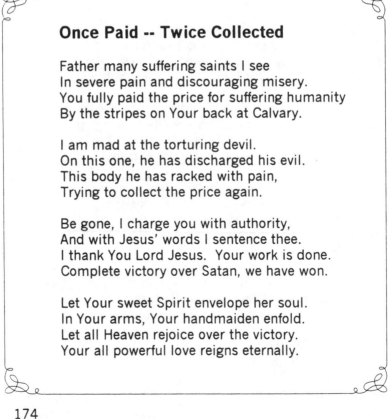

Once Paid -- Twice Collected

Father many suffering saints I see
In severe pain and discouraging misery.
You fully paid the price for suffering humanity
By the stripes on Your back at Calvary.

I am mad at the torturing devil.
On this one, he has discharged his evil.
This body he has racked with pain,
Trying to collect the price again.

Be gone, I charge you with authority,
And with Jesus' words I sentence thee.
I thank You Lord Jesus. Your work is done.
Complete victory over Satan, we have won.

Let Your sweet Spirit envelope her soul.
In Your arms, Your handmaiden enfold.
Let all Heaven rejoice over the victory.
Your all powerful love reigns eternally.

What Do We See

The world is staggering, nature is in a drastic upheaval.
Millions of souls are plunging into hell, led by the devil.
"Are God's children included in this great, great throng?"
'Yes, some are.' "Lord open our eyes to see what is going on!"
"What is God doing? Is He there sitting in a rocking chair
Watching humanity be swallowed up in death and despair?"

Remember Jesus told us that such things would surely come
And there would be no help to be had and nowhere to run.
Daniel had a panoramic view of what the end-time shall be.
He, a strong man, fainted at what he was permitted to see.
Prophets saw the last judgement worse than any hitherto.
Jeremiah said we'll consider it perfectly. His word is true.

'This I will cause them to know', twice He declares this word,
'They shall know the might of My hand. My name is the Lord'
Zephaniah tells of great darkness, fear and of bitter dismay,
He councils us to open our ears. Hear what God has to say.
Whole heartedly seek Him to be worthy to be hid in that day,
Sincerely repent.Let the Spirit show us the Jesus way to pray

The prophets saw something to the superlative degree
And longed to be here helping Jesus finish in victory.
God is prepared with power greater than Satan's display.
Together we shall bring in His harvest in a glorified way.
So glory in Him, feed on His word, see what He will do.
Trials are to transform us and His words, our minds renew.

This is the vision the Lord's kingdom will now fulfil.
His purpose will be accomplished, He shall perform His will.
Procrastination and hesitation hinders what He doth require.
Be steadfast, prompt, and obedient to fulfil Father's desire.
We are not doing it, but it is His glorious presence within.
Satan's domain is defeated. Christ's Body is destined to win.

Every prophesy has a near and far fulfilment.
Ezekiel is looking at the last judgement. With this in mind,
read what he says in the seventh chapter of his book.

Is the Word of God Really True?

Does the Word of God work? Is it really true?
Can it change situations for people like you?
Is it stronger than feeling, even severe pain,
Or sad confusion that bogs down the brain?

Will it stand when the stability is swept away?
And you look around you but there isn't a way.
No strength within, and you don't know what to do...
Can the Word of God help and make a way for you?

Yes, God's Word is final and settled forever.
Can His promises fail? No never, never, never!
Mary believed and said, "I know there shall be
A performance of the Word the Lord spoke to me."
                                        Luke 1:45
It'll change the black heart and make it white,
And bring out of darkness into marvellous light.
Thessalonians says it will work if we believe.
Regardless of our plight. It'll comfort and relieve.

Sickness, sin, sorrow and death, old Adam gave,
But Jesus restored all and He is able to save.
The world's sin He bore, in agony and pain,
So He could through us, ruin Satan's reign.

He is our wisdom, righteousness and power;
So we can be more than conquerors in this hour.
We must reckon ourselves dead to natural carnality,
To enjoy the Word and His loving reality.

Just receive what He gives with confidence,
And an eternal reward shall be your recompense.
Satan's words of doubt, do not think or say.
Declare faith for every case throughout the day.

He is the Supplier of His faith and His grace
That will prepare us for what's soon to take place.
We must repent, and with the whole heart seek Him,
To be cleansed and ready without and within.

176

We have no concept of the glory we'll receive,
If we claim His word and in His faith believe.
Its for eternity, not just a day or a night,
It is most important that the choice be right.

His mercy and wrath are of the same degree --
Either joy unspeakable, or likewise agony.
There'll be no changing of our eternal state.
Its best to change now, before its too late.

The Darkest Night Verses the Brightest Day

A horrible darkness does this world enshroud;
A bright light is shining. God is speaking loud.
Whoever has an ear to hear and a heart to obey,
Shall walk in the Lord's light in a glorified way.
We know darkness and light cannot agree;
When the light shines, darkness will flee.
Dense fog can nullify even bright light
But Satan can't obliterate God's light so bright.

This is God's time for Him to manifest
Satan's wickedness and His righteousness.
A mighty battle is now taking place:
Satan's army verses God's army of grace.
The glory of the Lord shall be seen world wide.
The world won't stand when God's wrath is applied.
God gave us a will; we're responsible to decide:
With Whom we shall stand, and with Whom we'll abide.

Those with a hearing ear and a heart to obey God's word
Repent of sin, and sincerely seek the Lord.
They shall manifest Father's power and His glory,
And cover the world with Salvation's story.
Then a world wide shocker will come for sure:
Those ready for Jesus won't be around any more.
Then God will make a speedy riddance of all sin
And the millennium of righteousness will usher in.

Blessing or Fate

Today is a time that is most momentous,
And it shall become exceedingly worse.
God's holy men, for years were faithful to tell,
Of a world wide financial collapse, a taste of Hell.

The Earth shall tremble when they see
With God their dealing, not humanity.
Terrible things that we look not for
Are coming to pass, more and more.

Only two sides are available for us to take.
If we choose the world, then God we'll forsake.
According to God's wrath decree,
So also is His love and His mercy.

Seek Him to be worthy to be hid that day.
Repent of your sin, and fast and pray.
A God given faith for us, Jesus brought,
Which is able to stand Satan's onslaught.

His faith is produced by standing on God's word.
It was proven in the great sufferings of our Lord.
It's coming! An unprecedented manifestation of His glory,
That quickly shall finish and fulfill Salvation's story.

With a holy boldness, His saints shall perform
His mighty acts, like when the Church was born.
Its the greatest manifestation of God in man,
To bring a glorious finish to His plan.

For those not ready, its only right I should say:
Some of what the word says, is coming your way.
'The spoiler shall suddenly come upon us.' 1
Woe betide us then, if in the Lord we do not trust.

'There will be a great shaking in Israel,' 2
And confidence in man shall utterly fail.
'Upon all men will I bring distress.' 3
Because they love sin and hated righteousness. 4
178

None shall be able to abide His indignation.' 5
And what they trusted in shall be desolation. 6
Humanity is blind to the reality of Hell, so they don't care.
No words can tell; no end to the agony they'll have to bear.

John, the beloved, fainted when given to see
The reality of the second death for eternity.
There is no reduction in Satan's ghastly reward.
I prefer to live and die for Jesus, my wonderful Lord.

'Woe to her that is filthy and polluted. She obeyed not
The Voice; she received not correction; She trusted not
In the Lord; She drew not near to her God.' 7
David said, 'The wicked are turned into Hell.' 8

'I saw the dead, small and great stand before God;
And the books were opened: and another book was opened,
Which is the Book of Life: and the dead were judged
Out of those things which were written in the books,
According to their works and whosoever was not found
Written in the Book of Life was cast into the lake of fire.' 9

---

1. Jeremiah 6:26   2. Ezekiel 38:19
3. Zephaniah 1:17   4. 1 Corinthians 2:13
5. Jeremiah 10:10   6. Zephaniah 1:18
7. Zephaniah 3:1,2   8. Psalm 9:17
9. Revelation 20:12, 15

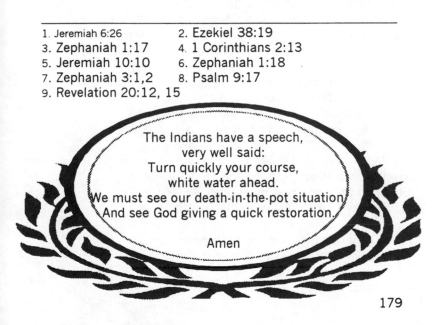

The Indians have a speech,
very well said:
Turn quickly your course,
white water ahead.
We must see our death-in-the-pot situation
And see God giving a quick restoration.

Amen

The Great Conflict

God created Lucifer as the son of the morning,
The top cherub, with power and beauty adorning.
Lucifer's pride caused him from Heaven to be expelled.
With one third of the angels, he was cast down to Hell. 1

Satan then transplanted that pride into man,
To destroy God's purpose in creation's plan.
Satan knew pride, to God was an abomination;
Thus he sealed up man in his condemnation.

Pride is the most dangerous sin of the soul,
It will open the door to demonic control.
It will keep us from God's riches, possession,
And make us lose out on His Spiritual refreshing.

God has weapons and armour, the foe to defeat;
For our protection, this armour is complete.
Seek His wisdom to apply it each day
To prepare for the battle coming our way.

The helmet of Salvation for us You bought,
To protect our minds from Satan's onslaught.
Our vain imaginations, dear Lord bring down
That Your righteousness our heads might crown.

On our shoulders in watchful prayer,
We minister to Your Body in loving care.
The breastplate of righteousness on us place,
That we may function in Your power and grace.

Wash our face, and make it shine,
That the world will know we are wholly Thine.
Surprise the people at what they will see,
So they will admit, we have been with Thee.

That from our belly a river shall flow,
And life will spring up wherever we go.
To do the work You planned for this day:
Grant wisdom, obedience and power for the way.
180

Gird up our loins with the Holy Word,
That our right hand can use that two edged sword.
And our left hand hold that protective shield,
To stop all the darts the devil will wield.

Grant our legs to firmly stand,
In the gap You've placed us, under Your command;
And demand the devil, who has jumped our claim,
To release our loved ones, in Jesus Name!

Clad our feet with Your gospel of grace,
That we be on time and in the right place.
As You did Your work, so let us do,
With our heart and eyes, solely fixed on You.

Like the fearless David, the weak shall stand 2
And be alert to Your command. 3
With the power of the Word the enemy they'll defeat,
And all of Satan's army will have to retreat.

When the temple was completed as You had planned,
Your glory was so bright, no man could stand.
Prepare us for this great visitation coming,
Or from Thy presence, we will find ourselves running.

This is God's word, which He is now fulfilling;
To stand in His ranks, are we truly willing?
To miss this visitation is an unrecoverable loss,
Ending in sorrow at the greatest cost.

---

1. Isaiah 14:13,14   2. Zechariah 12:8   3. Psalm 110:3

I read a good word in Second Corinthians 4:11.
It revived my spirit. From God it was given.
Death is working in this frail house of clay,
But Jesus' life in this mortal flesh, shall He display.

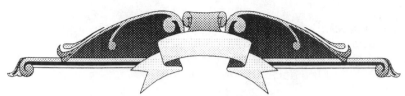

Humility and Pride

The more I learn, the more unsure of myself I feel.
An angel said, "Don this mantle. It will temper your steel."
Could such a plain mantle mark my rank?
Yes, being clothed with God's grace, for which we thank!

The highest rank in the eternal Kingdom is humility.
Don't move anywhere without it to experience great victory!
It is the weapon that puts the hike on the devil.
It hinders his most powerful method to establish his evil.

Satan's counter-attack is a weapon not easy to see.
Thousands of mighty warriors fall in defeat by this enemy.
They fail because they refuse the mantle of humility.
One by one they lay down the weapons of God's armoury.

The next enemy Satan puts forth is strong delusion.
It, with powerful pride, make a bad union.
They slyly slip in, the warriors don't even see,
Until they're utterly defeated, and lose the victory.

Pride is the worst enemy that causes God's people to fall.
No matter what height they attain, pride is fatal!
Diligently remember these things and you won't fall.
David said, "Abide under His wings, and on His name call!"

"Stay close to Me!", declares our ever-present Lord!
My joy, glory, grace, and love on you shall be poured!
Don't be side-tracked by what you go through.
Walk humbly with Me, and My will you will do!

Pride is such a ghastly thing;
People can be full of it,
and not even know it.

God Hates Sin

We need a revelation of sin today,
Where it is from, and its destiny.
Sin can never enter Heaven we know,
If we live in it, there's only one place to go.
It is not Father's will that anyone goes there.
Jesus bore the world's sin, to deliver from Hell's despair.
If we choose the flesh, we'll be filled with self-righteousness.
If our will is to live for God, we'll manifest His holiness.

The Bible warns about two deadly sins that damn the soul:
It is fornication and adultery in which the world does roll.
God sees adultery in field and on hill. He calls it abomination
And whoso doeth it, hasteneth his soul to destruction. [1,2]
Balam couldn't curse Israel, but Balac could corrupt them.
They chose adultery to bring God's people into great sin.
A prince's daughter into the Israeli camp went,
And a leader of God's people took her into his tent.

Aaron's grandson charged in and slew them with his sword,
And the plague was stayed by the Word of the Lord.
Moses taught God's people to hear and fear the Lord,
And be fully obedient to His Holy Word.
If anyone commits adultery they both must die, Moses said.
Today its' diseases are sweeping the world with dread.
In Romans, Paul pictures this sin very well; [3]
Its a steep, steep slide into the pit of Hell.

In the Bible from one end to the other we see,
God's wrath upon this sin without mercy.
In both Testaments we read: thou shalt not commit adultery
It is Satan's main plan to drag the world into his misery.
Destruction and misery will mark the way,
Of this type of living so manifested today.
It takes a quality decision, to be delivered from this thing.
It must be for the Lord, to prepare us for our heavenly King.

---

1. Jeremiah 13:27   2. Proverbs 6:32
3. Romans 1:24,26-29,32

Consider the Good -- Be Aware of the Bad

Great Blessings are for those who put their trust in Me.
Heaven's joys shall fill them, as water the sea.
To a condemned world they extend My mercy.
All who receive it shall also receive My glory.

An equal heir with Me they shall be,
Of Father's love and riches for eternity.
Cursed be those who on the flesh rely.
They depart from Me and shall bitterly cry.

No death is possible for the eternal soul;
Satan's reward shall be their goal.
It is not My will for them to go there.
I did all I could that agony to spare.

If in My Book their name is not written,
With My eternal judgement they shall be smitten.
Why not turn to Me now with all of your heart,
And from the world's corruption willingly depart?

Abhor that which is evil, cleave to that which is good.
Make no provision to fulfil the flesh lust, declares His Word.
We must stand to our feet and play the man,
A wishy-washy Christian cannot meet the demand.

Eternal despair, regret, remorse, and hopeless grief
Shall envelop the lost soul, with no relief.
I never pour out My judgement, but first My mercy.
To accept it means My blessings, riches and glory.

With your soul all shall be well.
You need not fear the devil's Hell.
Don't pass Me by to have your way.
When time ceases, it will not pay.

The Question God Is Solemnly Asking

Where will we go, when our short life is through?
Of all our earthly works, God will give His review.
Can our heart endure and our hands be strong on that day,
Every detail of life passes before us in a panoramic way?

The earth life ends, but the soul lives on for eternity;
This short life determines what our destiny shall be.
In the last days you'll consider it perfectly, the Lord says.
His broom of destruction, sweeps all our iniquities away.

A genuine cleansing there shall be,
Of the church and of all humanity.
One more time the world shall see,
The strength of My hand, and My glory.

A battle is raging in the spiritual realm,
God and His angels are at the helm.
A Body is being raised up through divine revelation,
Without fear, declaring His words with demonstration.

Repent with your whole heart. Listen to what I say,
To be worthy to be hidden from the coming fray.
Strong men shall weep and bitterly cry.
Multitudes shall suffer and suddenly die.

On one hand we see God's great power and glory,
While with the other He is ending sin's sad story.
Hell's mouth is open wide for many to fall in --
All those who chose their own way, and delighted in sin.

No flesh can stand before the awesome presence of our Lord,
Unless His righteous, sanctifying Spirit on them be poured.
Five virgins had no oil in their vessel. Their light did die.
The Bridegroom came and the door was shut. They did cry!

You have chosen the thing in which I have no delight,
So at the end of your sojourn you have lost the fight.
In hopeless regret, eternal grief and pain;
You'll sincerely long for a chance to decide again.

All night long you will repent in bitter tears.
There will be no answer, just ghastly fears.
No more of His tender mercy to forgive and restore.
What you now love, your soul shall then abhor.

Right now a great restoration is taking place,
There is a world-wide avalanche of God's saving grace.
All the enemy has taken, Jesus will restore to you,
If you cry to Him now, and long for His will to do!

Decided by the words of our mouth, is death or life.
We'll either walk in satanic darkness or heavenly light.
Let your words be few. Holy Spirit will tell you what to say.
Great love, joy, peace, and satisfaction shall flood your way!

God Speaks to My Heart

Oh My people, hearken diligently to My word
To be the people who do know their Lord.
Forgiveness, love, and mercy is the key
To bring you into oneness with Me.

If you refuse to forgive your brother,
In darkness and grief you shall wander
And miss the restoration you could have had
By justifying yourself with feelings so bad.

186

Don't grieve over what you are going through.
I am aware of the path I have chosen for you.
You must be emptied of self to be set free.
Your way isn't in the flesh. It is in Me.

If you long for the things in which I delight,
You will be brought from darkness into Light.
My love is so great -- it is beyond degree,
And it will bring you into oneness with Me.

Your ways are not My ways, or your thoughts My thoughts,
So repent and seek Me with all of your heart.
I want to give you all, not just a tiny part.
Unforgiveness and no mercy, shall block the way

Of being the people I'm calling you to be today.
Time is short, My beloved, open your eyes and see;
There is perfect confidence and harmony with Me,
And then I will do My exploits through thee.

I am not picking on you because of your hard state.
I just want you to fall into My arms and I'll undertake.
Put no confidence in the flesh, but put it all in Me.
The situations you are in are just to help you see:

Flesh profits nothing to manifest what I desire.
To be your constant delight is what I do require.
I know how to remove the dross and take away the tin
So do not grumble about the fires I put you in.

In everything give thanks, is My will for you.
Confidence in My word will bring you through.
You need My abundant rain to stand the test
Which is coming, with My quietness and rest.

My love in you shall then be revealed.
By My righteousness you shall be sealed
And ready for the soon coming glorious day,
When the mortal shall put on My immortality.

Don't Miss What's Happening!

The water gushes out of the rock that He clave
And it is flooding the world like a great tidal wave.
The walls are crumbling and barriers give way.
God's finishing work is now on display.
The saints are rejoicing, cleansed and set free.
God is pouring out His Spirit abundantly.
There's a voice from heaven -- the voice of His Son, 1
Calling all sinners, turn quickly and come. 2
Prisoners are coming forth from their cell; 3
His glorious Salvation rescues from Hell,
And a horrible life of sin and misery.
They heard His voice and He is setting them free.
Those who have fallen to the depths of sin
Are coming to Jesus, a new life to begin.
God is using them in an outstanding way --
In delivering the afflicted, and teaching to pray.
He is fulfilling His word and it surely shall be;
Glory covers the Earth as waters the sea.
Unbelieving eyes shall be open so wide --
They will regret His word they have denied. 4, 5
A very quick work, the Lord will make -- 6
Then up goes the Bride, and shut goes the gate. 7
A great broom will sweep with destruction and woe;
They'll be so sad that they're not ready to go.
All nations shall quake and severely tremble -- 8
Their treasured possessions shall fall and crumble.
Great fear and distress shall flood over their soul,
And their overtaxed minds shall go out of control. 9

---

1. Psalms 50:1   2. Zephaniah 2:2,3   3. Isaiah 42:7
4. Zephaniah 1:6   5. Psalms 28:5   6. Romans 9:28
7. Matthew 25:10   8. Zephaniah 1: 14-18 9. Luke 21:26

Jesus wants a Revival

Jesus wants a revival and it surely shall be--
A Heaven-sent revival of fire and purity.
His Spirit is searching for you and for me,
And He's placed a desire in us for His equity.

With a purging fire, He is visiting us today,
So all of our dross and tin, He can take away.
Our stumbling blocks of pride and carnal show,
In this cleansing fire, will all have to go.

To be His loving, obedient, overcoming Counterpart,
Governed by His word, which is His heart --
This holy desire, from Heaven came:
To be a people to glorify His name.

His power frightened His disciples, we see.
They cried out when He calmed the wind and the sea.
Do we want this revival? Are we willing to pay the price?
We must be cleansed to offer a pure sacrifice.

Is His maturity in us, our only goal?
Are our hearts burdened for the dying soul?
Our Bridegroom is coming, our Almighty King,
For His purified Bride, His beloved Queen.

If we are not ready, we will bow and back out,
And miss the greatest demonstration, He's bringing about.
That would be the saddest choice we could make;
The same side as the great bear, we would take.

We must give up our thinking of how things should be done.
God will not consult us -- how His business is run.
A total surrender with repentance it will take,
But an eternity of rejoicing, it will surely make.

God's Call to Attention

"Tremble thou Earth at the presence of the Lord"
Now showing His people the power of His word.
The works of His hands are judgement and verity
That shall stand fast, now and for eternity.

From the rising of the sun, to the going down of the same,
Eyes are opening as God's mighty works make fame.
Saints are rejoicing, praising and worshipping the Lord.
Through His wonderful redemption, they are restored.

"Tremble thou Earth at the presence of the Lord"
Very soon His great wrath on all sin will be poured.
For a short time, His mercy and blessing shall fall like rain
To prepare all who will, against that hour of great pain.

Their hearts shall be fixed, established, trusting in the Lord
In the power of His Spirit and His omnipotent word.
Fear and darkness shall not make them afraid --
The weak shall be strong when evils against them raid.

The fear of the Lord protects from all evil.
The power of His Spirit and word, puts to flight the devil.
This is a most glorious visitation that has come to man;
Lord, grant us a longing heart to fit into Your plan.

This visitation will be short, there is no time for delay.
If we do not desire to fear the Lord and go His way,
Our inner man shall writhe in deep regret,
And our loss, we shall never ever forget.

Missing the Mark

Revelation 7: 14 to 17
Luke 19:42-44

Are we missing the mark of our visitation
Being absorbed in fleshly preoccupation?
God has made great provision for our peace today,
But from the world, peace is totally taken away.

Ghastly fears loom up on every side.
Evident war warnings now are world wide.
God's happy people, worldly attractions release.
Their eyes are open to what belongs to their peace.

The enlightened word has become alive again.
They learned the secret of letting Jesus reign.
Troubles and problems will surely come
That will be impossible to bear alone.

In it all, they'll know in their spirit,
The Yahweh Jehovah God in them can do it.
His love, wisdom, discernment and grace
Shall be their sufficiency in any place.

The world shall see it, and could partake
If they obeyed, and the preparation make.
So empty yourself of every fleshly aim.
Open wide your mouth for the latter rain.

It will enable His Bride to stand true
When His wrath and power is witnessed by you.
A world wide shocker shall suddenly take place:
A mass missing of those filled with His grace.

People will cry for loved ones who won't be there,
And will recall their words and intercessory prayer.
God has a plan: Refuse the Antichrist mark to take.
Prefer great suffering and the death he will make.

A great reward shall be given unto them
'Washed and made white in the blood of the Lamb'.
No more hurts or tears to fall.
One with Jesus, their all in all.

A World-Wide Revelation

Rick Berry gives a prophetic word on God's end-time plan,
And tells us to prepare for this grace that is to come to man.
In the bosom of Christ's Body is a longing for intimacy,
And a yearning to bring forth His oneness in love and unity.

In a universal way, God is giving the world something to see:
His victorious army stands in love, and great expectancy.
Father is well aware of their needs and their state,
And is renewing their wineskins for this last great mandate.

Many gifts He is giving in music, art and poetry
That express His will in beautiful simplicity.
Thousands gather letting the drama of God's heart flow;
All sin and bondages of the flesh, they let go -- they let go.

Preaching the Kingdom gospel with restoration.
In loving loyalty, His work they are manifesting.
A very quick work in righteousness they shall do;
According to Romans 9:28, it shall be through.

Awesome praise and worship ascend from many a place,
And a hunger to be filled with God's love and grace.
This is the greatest harvest that ever has been,
And in a world-wide way His glory shall be seen.

If we reject the Light, we will walk in the dark;
So let us open our eyes and open wide our heart.
The sides are being chosen. We're being lined up.
We're making our choice. We'll drink of which cup?

Walls are coming down and unity is quickly growing.
Churches coming together, the like has not been known.
The Church Jesus left was filled with love, power, and glory.
He'll return for a like Church that has finished the story.

It is Jesus Who is leading His chosen, cleansed army,
And willingly they follow Him all of the way.
Suddenly the trumpet will sound and it shall be --
Jesus presents to Father, His Bride in excellency.
192

The New Year

Perilous times greet this new year.
Its a time of sorrow, debt, sickness and fear.
From the beginning of time, Satan has worked his plan,
To conscript world force and humanity into his hand.

Now he has people where he wants them to be
To bring forth his evil debauchery
There's no limit to the depth man will go into evil --
On every side we see the corruption of the devil.

There is a great spiritual force hindering his plan:
God is bringing forth His army of yielded, cleansed man.
Every possible device is aimed to bring them down;
Jesus is their Captain; louder and louder is their song.

Demons are trembling as their strongholds give way --
As God's sons stand together to fast and to pray.
Their heart longing is with the Father to be one,
To bring a good finish to the work the first church begun.

A mighty conflict is well on its way:
But God's army shall be prepared for this day.
A severe persecution may soon arise,
To push us in or out -- no compromise.

We need to see now what soon shall be,
And earnestly prepare for His power and glory,
By being freed from materialistic society,
And invest our all in this battle for eternity.

Procrastination

I said to Marge, "I'm going to write about procrastination."
She said, "Oh no, not today. Just enjoy your relaxation"
I have decided to read my Bible and fast and pray.
There are priorities, so guess I'll leave it for Saturday.

O no I can't do that -- that *is* procrastination.
According to the Bible, that road leads to condemnation.
Lord open my eyes and let me see:
How this deadly sin wants to engulf me.

I think I had better check my lifestyle with the Word.
Does my appearance, words and actions glorify my Lord?
It is so easy to let godless society contaminate the heart:
Ape it's style, lust, and pride; and wicked T.V. has a part.

On that crucial church debt, I'll do my part; but not today.
First there are other things I want to get cleared away.
But, here is something in Matthew 6 and 33:
If I seek His Kingdom first, He will look after me.

I've heard say, Haggai is a small but a practical Book,
So I will flip over there and have a look:
Chapter 1 and verse 9: What I have He will blow away!
Because the great need of His house I neglect today.

Lord, I'm in a dilemma and don't know what to do.
'Just do what I say and I will work all things out for you.'
'I want a people of joy, who fear, love and pray;
With a keen ear to hear My Word and a willing heart to obey.'

Lord, I do have a problem, in which I see no way,
But if Your presence goes with me, it will be O.K.
You're not poverty stricken. There's no end to You're grace.
At Your appointed time, things will fall into place.

'If you simply trust and happily release your burdens to Me
My blessings will run after you abundantly,
But you must be alert and ready to move,
And I will flood your soul with My peace, joy, and love.'
194

I love You Lord. You're so forgiving and sweet.
My ashes I lay at your nail scarred feet.
Together we will make it, You and I;
I'm longing to see You come down through the sky!

Its no time now to procrastinate.
His coming is so quick, I'd surely be late.
I must be alert and eager to obey.
Procrastination is of Satan -- so get out of my way!

Are You Ready?

We must change our selfish attitude
Toward the Lord -- for loving gratitude.
He bore all the pain and misery of Hell for us
And made a way to eternal bliss -- How glorious!

Gabriel is ready with his trumpet, waiting to blow.
With a shout -- the sky will roll back like a scroll.
Those who are ready for Jesus, in a flash shall be gone.
What will be left? Just a pile of clothes they had on.

She'll not be lukewarm, continually sinning;
She'll be without spot, ready for the wedding.
God is positioning us for this final hour
And manifesting through us His glory and power.

Are you in a weak anaemic powerless condition?
Jesus is waiting to give you a great restoration.
God is getting us ready for the final countdown.
If you're headed the wrong way, please turn around.

Suddenly it will happen, so don't delay.
If you're not ready, it will be a sad, sad day;
So get oil in your vessel and oil in your lamp.
Be happy in Jesus, and shine in your camp.

End time prophesies are fulfilled in rapid succession.
Our Lord shall accomplish His purpose to this generation.
We are listening for the shout of the archangel --
Are your ears open, and tilted on this angle?

What Next?

Shadows are gathering, and black clouds arise;
A fearful foreboding is overtaking the skies.
Panic is seizing the human heart;
They grope like the blind in the dark.

We are entering the time when the angel shall cry, "Woe!"
Distressed humanity shall not know where to go.
Great rains are falling, floods cover the land.
Death and destruction are witnessed on every hand.

Many are standing together to help their fellow man,
Even though the tragedies are many, they do what they can.
The earth is trembling, hearts everywhere quake;
They heed not God's call their sin to forsake.

Even the Church, God's cleansing and judgment shall see;
The Lord is preparing His Bride in holiness and equity.
Light shall arise in the darkness, declares the Word,
For those who heartily forsake sin and follow the Lord.

There is a fearful division now taking place,
Separating those appointed to wrath from those to grace.
Our decision is to heed or reject God's last great cry:
Do we prefer death to life, and in our sin to die?

Destruction has no mercy if our heart we do not prepare.
Good intentions will not save us, or divert the despair.
We must open our ears and hear what God has to say,
About being worthy to be hidden from His wrath in that day.

"Let me be weighed in an even balance,
that God may know mine integrity."
Job 31:6

Get Ready Its Coming

The mighty God, even the Lord hath spoken and called 1
The whole earth to come and give up their all.
Terrorizing situations are soon to take place; 2
You will never stand without His wisdom and grace.
Many, many Christians' brooks will dry up,
Pride and self-righteousness only give an empty cup. 3
A great deluge from glory, God is about to outpour. 4
It will be too holy for uncleansed temples to endure.
Unto the upright, Light in the darkness shall arise, 5
And give the unprepared a big surprise.
Envy shall enter hearts because My exploits they can't do;
Such darkness shall envelop them, light won't shine through.
The great conflict of tomorrow is coming our way. 6
Joel says, rend your hearts not your garments; fast and pray;
Sanctify a solemn assembly and cry unto the Lord, 7
For a mighty destruction is coming, declares His Word. 8

Many shall not drink of the Spirit's great flow,
Because their pride and selfishness they cannot let go. 9
My coming is sudden, no time then to prepare. 10
In the great wedding supper, they shall not share. 11
Open your spiritual eyes, My loved ones and see
My loving compassion is reaching out to thee. 12
Give up your all, I'll give you much more -- 13
My wisdom for the righteous, I've laid up in great store. 14
If you earnestly seek Me, it is also for you. 15
Be My clean, yielded vessel that I may work through. 16
I've conquered the enemy, brought his force to naught 17
That a glorious victory for you could be wrought. 18
Rejoice in the trials and testings that come. 19, 20
They are preparing you for this last great run.
Keep your eyes on Me, I know what to do. 21
I am your Omnipotent God Who can take you through. 22

1.Psalms 50:1 2.Isaiah 10:3 3.Proverbs 16:5 4.James 5:7
5.Psalms 112:4 6.Isaiah 60:2 7.Joel 1:13-15 8.Isaiah 10:3
9.Proverbs 3:7 10.Revelation 3:10,11 11.Matthew 25:11,12
12.John 17:23 13.Matthew 19:29 14.Prov 2:7 15.Prov 2:4-6
16.Isaiah 52:11 17. I John 3:8 18.Rom. 8:37 19.James 1:2
20. 1 Peter 1:7 21. Psalms 112:7 22. Jude 23:24   197

The Antichrist is Here

The Antichrist is here and boldly declares his aim.
His name is Juan Carlos. He is the King of Spain.
Jack van Impie says he fulfills all Bible prophesy:
A man of great intelligence, meeting the necessity.

This man of great potential is a Roman end-time King;
Promising peace; to solve problems, and restore everything.
His declarations surely open our eyes.
As to his identity, he does not disguise.

'I am the king of Jerusalem. I hear your despairing cry.
I'm your longed for messiah, for whom you would die.
I'll bring about the peace this world is crying for,
And I will be received as their mighty conqueror.'

'No other messiah is coming. I am your king and lord.
Your desires shall be granted when peace I've restored.
The Gentile rule is finished. It is over.
I am king, the world's chosen dictator.'

The eyes of the world are upon this man.
'Be he god or devil, rule us he surely can.'
All that the Word says, Carlos is saying today,
But the Lord's elect is hindering his way.

Jesus will oblige him and call home His own,
Then Carlos will ascend his end-time throne.
The world is being visited with God's saving grace,
And Jesus' end-time harvest is quickly taking place.

Jesus said His harvest shall suddenly be gathered in,
Then He will rapture His Bride from this world of sin.
Right now we are making our decision, both you and I,
For whom we'd stand and for whom we would die.

An awesome preparation Jesus is now fulfilling,
He is purging His own with a great cleansing.
If we are not purified we shall not be able to stand,
The joy and glory He is pouring into His prepared man.

It is our decision. Are we satisfied with what we've got?
Are our hearts crying to Jesus to cleanse every spot?
Are we longing for our glorified Christ to behold?
Are we accepting the fires to purify our gold?

No matter how high the degree, Jesus is in control.
Carefully He is bringing forth His image in our soul;
So He can present to Father in the greatest ecstasy,
His Bride adorned in His beauty, love, joy, and glory.

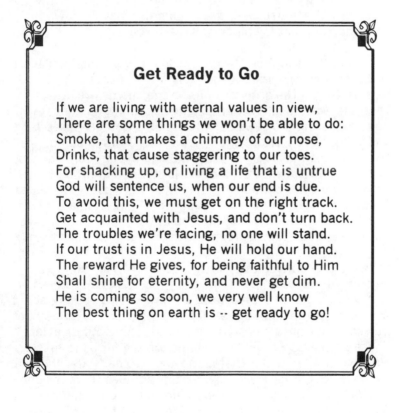

Get Ready to Go

If we are living with eternal values in view,
There are some things we won't be able to do:
Smoke, that makes a chimney of our nose,
Drinks, that cause staggering to our toes.
For shacking up, or living a life that is untrue
God will sentence us, when our end is due.
To avoid this, we must get on the right track.
Get acquainted with Jesus, and don't turn back.
The troubles we're facing, no one will stand.
If our trust is in Jesus, He will hold our hand.
The reward He gives, for being faithful to Him
Shall shine for eternity, and never get dim.
He is coming so soon, we very well know
The best thing on earth is -- get ready to go!

God's Round-Up Time is Now

We are in the last chapter of human history
Which shall usher in the never ending eternity.
God placed humanity in a three part identity:
Natural, spiritual, and carnal -- each marked in clarity.
The Lord said He would make a speedy riddance of sin,
So the Millennium and His Kingdom of Peace can come in.
The natural is void of eternal life and desire for God;
The spiritual walk in humble obedience with their Lord;
The carnal neglected their light, so darkness it became.
No light, they were not ready when the Bridegroom came.
In horrifying anguish, very great suffering they'll know.
'You shall die, but My blood will wash you whiter than snow.'

There are three gatherings the Lord is now putting in place:
All Satan's army verses Jesus' holy army of sovereign grace.
He's gathering His army to pour on the enemy great wrath,
Then the world shall reel and stagger in that ghastly bath.
He is gathering the Jews back to Jacob's God-promised land
And bringing His Bride together with the Jews to stand.
To annihilate these two groups, the enemy has well planned,
But the Yahweh Jehovah God has for them a great surprise.
With Him they're contending, and their dead everywhere lies.
Those who have mocked and laughed saying:'It is a big fake'
Shall eat their words when the cup of God's wrath they take,
But those in our Lord's mighty army will a great finish make.

"When you see these things begin to be manifested,
Rejoice, lift up your heads, for soon you shall be raptured."
The world is full of destructions with new ones coming about
Wise men at the helm are saying, we find there is no way out
Our compass needle is spinning, and spelling out disaster.
These problems we will face will be too big for us to master.
We have spotted a star that is moving. To earth it will come.
We have sought for a way to divert it, but alas there is none.
Revelation 8:8 says a fiery mountain will be cast into the sea.
This time is utterly shocking. There will be no place to flee.
The water will be blood and bitter as wormwood. This is why
A third of the fish, birds, animals, and also people will die.

They'll cry, 'Mountains hide us from the wrath of the Lamb'.
This is so appalling, none shall be able to stand.
Jesus is pleading, repent. With all of your heart seek Me
To be worthy to be hidden. I'll forgive and set you free.
Now all the soldiers of Jesus must leap to their feet
And in His loving compassion, rescue His wandering sheep.

We're being lined up, there's no time to waste,
If you want to receive His loving grace.
It will be worth it all when we see what we've missed,
And we will be with Jesus our Saviour in eternal bliss.

The Church Age Ends

"He that believeth not the Son shall not see life;
But the wrath of God abideth on him."   John 3:36b

Right now the world is experiencing an amazing transition.
It's God's time to manifest this outstanding transaction:
Put Satan where he belongs. Make a speedy riddance of sin,
Thus preparing the way to usher the Millennium in.
God's plan, purpose, and goal He'll accomplish by His Spirit.
He needs a specially prepared humanity to do it;

And He uses the man Satan ruined with his wickedness
To totally defeat Satan in all his deceitfulness.
This is God's greatest manifestation of Himself in man.
If we're not counted here we'll be conscripted in Satan's plan
There is a hunger in God's people to get into His word,
Receive of His wisdom and understanding, declares the Lord.

The longing of their soul is for Father's Kingdom to come
And in every detail, His perfect will to be done.
The awesome holiness of God, they are beginning to realize,
And are performing His mighty works before our eyes.

201

This is the answer to the heart's deep longing,
To be one with Jesus in the work He is doing.
For the privilege of this hour they'll greatly rejoice,
But woe to those who have made the wrong choice.
These are the works now being revealed:
The dead raised, the bound set free, the sick healed.

Romans 9:28 says: God will quickly finish His perfect plan,
Then He'll rapture His saints, His purified man. 1
We are now coming in on the last round of the race.
We'll receive either God's great wrath or His great grace.
We are seeing these things quickly coming to pass,
And the wide-eyed world is standing aghast.

There never was a time when God moved as He is today.
He is giving His servants a clear revelation of His way.
Anyone who wants God, He'll give them grace to stand.
He will teach them His word and His plan.
No words can tell the agony those not ready shall bear
If they refuse the Antichrist and his judgment not share.

The requirement for His Bride now is maturity; 2
When we are one with Christ, the world will see our victory.
God has given us power to meet His demand. 3
Regardless of all Satan's onslaught, the Bride shall stand.
Man's day is over. God is now in command, 4
And those who dare to oppose Him shall never stand. 5

It's just the beginning but just wait and you will see
The full manifestation of His power is yet to be.
Through revelations we are getting glimpses in the Spirit. 6
That's why there must be a cleansing of vessels to contain it.
"There is nothing hidden that shall not be revealed." 7
In a world wide way man will have no excuse. 8

Read Ephesians 1: 4, 5, 6; and Jude verse 14, 15, and 24.

---

1. 1 Thessalonians 4:16,17   2. Ephesians 4:13
3. John 17: 21,22   4. 2 Peter 1: 3, 4
5. Matthew 16: 18b   6. Matthew 9:17
7. Matthew10:26   8. Romans 1: 20

A Transition Now in Action

A great transition is now taking place:
From the early church until now is the Age of Grace.
Jesus said: In His appointed time this Age would pass away.
The signs He gave, quickly are being fulfilled today.

It is God's moving time, and He is ushering in
The next great Age, which is called the Millennium.
He made this earth once, and He will make it again
With the removal of all sin, suffering, and pain.

Before this great feature can come to pass,
There's a restoration which forever, shall last.
The broom of God's wrath will make a speedy riddance of sin
Satan will be utterly defeated, and all who follow him.

It will take seven years for God to pour out His wrath.
Man will be utterly defeated, and lose all he hath.
Silver and gold will be no good on that day;
It will be dumped on the street, uselessly.

For a time, the Antichrist shall rule and prevail.
All who refuse to follow him, he will cruelly kill.
Suddenly the earth shall open before their eyes.
The Antichrist, beast, and false prophet, into Hell dives.

A special place for all who kill God's children, He prepared.
For a thousand years, Satan will join them there.
A blissful rule our Lord will usher in:
A Kingdom of righteousness, and putting away of all sin.

The victorious saints with Christ shall reign.
Their greatest joy will be for their greatest pain.
Then the white throne judgement comes to pass:
All not found in the Book of Life, into Hell are cast.

It's not God's will for us to go to that hellish pit.
Jesus took all the agonies of Hell, to deliver us from it.
The new Heaven and Earth shall completely fill
In the lost and redeemed man, His perfect will.

We'll see the price Jesus paid to set us free.
And we'll praise Him for the blood He shed, for eternity.
But the lost shall regret in hopeless grief,
In a horrible eternal Hell, with no relief.

They'll see what they missed, and wail in their plight.
If they could choose again, they would choose right.
They would listen to what God's word has to say,
And get prepared for this last great day.

Jeremiah said "Consider your latter end.", and twice he
Said "In the last day, you will consider it perfectly."

Repentance

In dense darkness the world situation was grim.
Satan had tricked God's children into great sin.
No help for the blind, bound, poor, sick and lame;
An evil spirit of hopelessness had the reign.
The time of manifesting God's great grace had come.
Five strange people chosen through whom it would be done.

A dedicated young maiden and a dear old sanctified woman.
A husband, a powerful preacher, and a godly old man.
This group together opened the door for the King of Kings;
The fulfilment of prophecy a babe in the manger brings.
What a strange setting for the greatest story ever told,
When the unfathomable love of God began to unfold.

In the Father's time all things were in place.
A wild, fiery, preacher announces God's amazing grace.
Repent, repent was his powerful theme.
Make ready, make ready for the King of Kings.

He is the Lamb of God, anointed to bring to birth,
To manifest and establish God's Kingdom in earth.
John's message of repentance and complete turning from sin
Was the needed preparation to bring Father's Kingdom in.
Two thousand years later the situation is still the same.
Not just one man but a holy army does proclaim:

"Repent, repent, its a precious gift from God in Jesus name!"
To make ready a holy people to manifest our Lord's fame.
At His first coming prophesies were fulfilled in every line.
At His second coming it also shall be; He'll come on time.
This precious Spirit of repentance is sweeping the universe.
Its so powerful to enable God to deliver all from the curse.

We must earnestly desire and fervently seek
For this Godly repentance over our sinful soul to sweep.
It will bring us into a loving unity with the Father,
And flood us with His joy, power, and grace for this hour.
Jesus uses this type of repentance to perform His work in us,
So we can face Satan's power in confidence and trust.

We must not grieve or dodge this powerful work of the Spirit.
Wholly respond to His leading that we may bear the fruit of it
To miss today's visitation, and not hear God's last call,
Will cause millions into horrible Hell to suddenly fall.
Jesus is calling, "Repent, repent, turn now to Me!
I've no desire for you to receive Hell's eternal agony!"

You did not appoint man to wrath, but to obtain
This great Salvation, in Jesus' name.
We dare not quench the Spirit and stubbornly reject
This great work God in us longs to perfect.

The Seven Trumpets

Revelation 8:2, 6-13; 9:1-6; 10:5-7)

Seven angels are ready their trumpets to sound
Announcing God's great wrath so soon will abound.
The first angel blows fearfully loud --
Down comes great hail and fire mingled with blood.

Nature is the first to drink of this awful cup;
One third of the trees and grass is burned up.
The second angel then sends forth his blast:
A great mountain of fire into the sea is cast,

A third part of the sea to blood is then turned,
A third part of the creatures die; a third of the ships burn.
The third angel sounds, and judges the water supply:
One third shall be so bitter, so many shall die.

The fourth angel blows: sun, moon and stars he will strike;
One third of the day becomes black as the night.
The fifth angel cries loudly `Woe, woe, woe'
Because of the great sorrow, the unsaved shall now know.

To the bottomless pit this angel has the key;
He opens it and a great black smoke shall they see.
Out of that smoke great locust shall appear
To torture the wicked for almost half a year.

God places a seal on His people against this hour
So these scorpion like stings on them have no power.
On all without the seal -- alas, alas
They'll seek for death, but it them shall pass.

These queer locusts had the stinger in their tail
And for five long months they will cause man to wail.
Sixth angel blows: two hundred thousand horsemen appear
To slaughter people for an hour, a week, a month and a year.
206

The seventh angel came and stood on the land and the sea:
He raised his hand toward Heaven: 'Time no longer shall be!'
He is announcing the mystery of God shall be finished;
Not one word that has been spoken shall be diminished.

All the prophets and Jesus spoke much about this day
When all sin and iniquity will be swept away.
If we love and hang on to our sin, out with it we will go.
What has been prepared for Satan, the lost will surely know.

In loving compassion Jesus asks us to consider our end.
Our decision determines where eternity we will spend.
A glorious restoration our Lord did provide
To present to the Father, the Lamb's spotless Bride.

Is There a Hell?

Some Finns Norwegians and Russians had a machine to bore
A hole through Earth's crust, its very depths to explore.
They rigged up a device to pick up any sound
That would give them a clue as to what they had found.

Nine miles down, something happened right then --
There was no more earth and the auger did spin.
In the bowels of the Earth, God said is Hell
And the screams of the lost, they heard very well.

Their very souls it did petrify --
The reality of Hell, they could not deny.
Out of that hole, fiendish demons did appear
And they fled for their lives in horrible fear.

When Russia heard it, they were very upset
And paid a large sum telling them their shock to forget.
Such an alarming feature so troubled their soul --
To hold it back, they had no control.

It finally hit the Norwegian press --
The rate it travelled, you could easily guess.
Into Brother Shamback's hands this account did fall.
He gave it to the host of T.B.N., whose name is Paul.

He had heard it before, but over the air, he read it again.
Brother Shamback preached, and he preached very plain:
'I believe in Hell, not because of what these men declare,
But because of what Jesus many times did share.'

He said a rich man died and in Hell lifted his eyes,
And unto Father Abraham, beseechingly cries:
'Please send Lazarus to give me a little sip
Of water to cool my tongue and my burning lip.'

'Son, I know the misery you are going through;
A great gulf is between us, so there's nothing I can do.'
'Then please send Lazarus, my brothers to tell
That they end not up in this awful Hell.'

'The prophets and Jesus they would not receive --
Even if Lazarus went back, they wouldn't believe.'
In Hell there's no water nor a breath of fresh air;
But an endless eternity of grief and despair.

Would you like to know how to escape a furnace like this?
'Get taken up with Jesus now. You'll enjoy heavenly bliss.'
Jack Hayford said 'Mother, how can I know
When Jesus comes back, if I'd be ready to go?'

'Before I answer that, son, I'd like to pray.
I'll give you your answer, but wait a day.'
'Son', said Mother, 'I have the answer you wished to know:
Get taken up with Jesus now, then with Him you will go!'

208

A Story
That Changed Lives

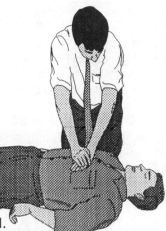

I read a story I want to tell
Of a nice man who went to Hell.
He was likeable, outgoing, congenial.
The sort of chap you'd like for a pal.

He loved his family. To his wife he was true.
In the natural, good deeds he tried to do.
He visited his doctor, fell dead on the floor,
And experienced the reality beyond death's door.

The good doctor and nurses through resuscitation
Brought him back and were shocked at his conversation.
A terrified look of alarm was mapped on his face --
Pupils dilated, hair stood on end; strange things took place.

I'm in Hell! I'm in Hell! I'm in Hell -- don't you know!
When you stop what you are doing, back into Hell I go.
The doctor frustrated at the look on his face
Shouted "Quiet --until I get this pacemaker in place!"

'To stay out of Hell, what shall I do?'
I guess pray and ask Jesus to save you!
'I don't know how to pray. You pray for me. Pray!'
I'm a doctor, not a preacher. I don't know what to say.

He screamed 'Pray for me! You've got to pray!'
The frantic doctor sought for words to say.
Feverishly working there on the floor,
Did for the man, a prayer outpour:

"Lord Jesus, I ask You to keep me out of Hell.
Save my soul and forgive my sin.
If I die, take me to heaven. If I live,
I'll be on your hook forever. Amen."

The patient stabilized and was sent to the I.C.U.
Dr. Rawlings went home; he knew what he'd do.
To make a search, he then decreed;
Very carefully he would proceed.

The mystery after death, he would pursue.
He'd find out if what the Bible said was true.
He would go see his friend and ask of him,
What that place was like he had been in.

He took down his Bible and read and read
To see if there was an afterlife for the dead.
Then went to see his patient friend
To find out what really happened.

He couldn't recall one thing he had seen,
Or the reality of the Hell to which he had been.
In detail the doctor explained what he displayed.
He had forgotten all but the prayer they prayed.

Both realized there was a stark reality
Where the lost shall spend eternity.
It changed their life; it changed their goal.
They learned the value of a lost soul.

The patient, not a preacher does faithfully tell,
'Friends get ready -- There is a hell!'
Doctor Rawlings wrote a book: "Beyond Death's Door".
Everywhere it goes, lives are changed o'er and o'er.

He authentically pictures the life hereafter,
And the book has become life's best seller;
So pick up a copy and drink it in.
Turn to Jesus, and turn from your sin.

A Poem on Mary Kathryn Baxter's Visit to Hell

Jesus said,"Kathryn, Father has chosen you to come with Me
on a journey through Hell, so you can know and see it.
My Spirit shall reveal and help you tell, what it means to be
sentenced to an eternal Hell." "I'll hold your hand,
strengthen and bring you through, and what you see shall be
written indelibly on you. You are to write a book and let the
world know the awful Hell to which all unbelievers shall go."

"The book you write of these revelations I give to you shall
turn many to Me when they see what the lost go through. I
plead for mercy, My heart groans to see them go that way.
They rush blindly to destruction, deaf to what My Spirit does
say." "I've done all I can to save the world from the pit of
despair. This book you will write shall turn many from
there." For days I prayed and dedicated to Him my life.
Suddenly, my room filled with an awesome light...

God's presence was so peaceful and joyful; and Love's strong
power --Never had I known it as I did in that hour. My spirit
left my body, we went through the sky. Jesus was so full of
glory and power I wanted to cry. "Don't be afraid, I love you,
with Me you are safe. Stay close as I reveal what shall take
place." I saw over the world dirty looking funnels that spun
both ways. "What are these?" I gasped, as they met my
gaze. "They are the gateways to Hell. We are about to take
one." Instantly we were there, our downward course began,
into a dark tunnel spinning like a top; the horrible stench
and darkness gave me a shock.

Invisible forces were moving there, ushering many into the awful pit of despair. Holding tightly to Jesus's hand, I cried, "Lord, what are these?" "Evil spirits to be spewed out on the world at Satan's release." Suction drew us forth, in shock I let out a cry! Big ugly snakes went slithering by. "I will give you strength and protection as we go through Hell. You must see and understand all, I will enable you to tell."

Horrible objects were darting here and there. Groaning sounds and wailing cries filled the filthy air. The path we walked was dry, powdery dirt. I could feel the despair. My senses were very alert. Scenes too awful for me to describe. No words would come for me to scribe.

Let me warn you, don't go to that ghastly place of excruciating pain and sorrow -- no way to erase. It's a place of grief beyond human belief, from which God faithfully warns there is no relief. "Wake up the watchmen! Let them faithfully tell My gospel to those who are heading for Hell!" "It's the Father who is speaking to you. We two are one. Be ever loving and forgiving, and follow Me. Now come." Each step I took was more horrible than the one before. Inexpressible dangers loomed up and more. Grateful for Jesus' protection, my heart cried, "Father help me do Thy will, through this experience your purpose fulfil." We stepped out of a tunnel into a wider place. There were numberless pots which we did face.

Hell is shaped like a body. "We are now seeing Hell's left leg. Each pot contains a lost soul which continually begs, "Let me out! Let me out! I sincerely repent; because of the life I lived, to this Hell I've been sent!" They were four feet by three feet and shaped like a bowl. The interior glowed like a red hot coal. In the middle was a poor lost soul kindled in flame. A rushing wind would envelop them in flames again. So many, many pits my heart ached to see, such a multitude of lost souls for eternity. They were just skeleton forms that could see, hear, talk, cry; yet the home of an eternal soul that never could die. I looked at a poor woman. "Can't we pull her out? Dear Lord, do!" With tearful eyes of compassion He had to say, "No."

Decayed flesh hung shredded dropping to the bottom of the pit. Her hair was gone, her nose and eyes were just empty sockets. "Her cries of repentance are too late to heed. Judgement is set, her eternal destiny decreed. We made man with a will to decide, whom he would serve and with whom he would abide. The way was clear if they were willing to see; the way of life, My child, is only in Me. The sentence was written in words clear and bold. They were willingly deaf and blind so the truth could not hold."

A man cried, "Forty years I've suffered in this fire! Isn't that enough to pay for my sin in this hellish mire?" "All mockers and unbelievers shall have their place in the fiery lake! You laughed and refused to believe. Now there is no escape. I gave him many calls. He would not believe. My message of grace he refused to receive." The angry man's words were blasphemous and foul as the flames engulfed his poor lost soul.

"Judgement and Hell have a stark reality. Many frightful things you have yet to see. Tell the world it is not My will for them to come here. It is filled with satanic forces, deadly suffering and fear."

I watched an eighty year old woman. She made my heart sad. Big worms crawled out of that bony skeleton, so bad, so bad! Jesus said, "All their earthly feelings are here intensified, and their memory forever with them shall abide. This one became bitter. Because of cancer pain she blamed and hated Me. I called her repeatedly, but she would not heed My plea. The ones I sent to help her she would not receive so she came to this place because she refused to believe.

This one heard My call and said, "Someday I'll come. Now I'm enjoying my fun." Her listening was too late, so to this place she has come. "Oh I wish I had listened to you ! " She lamentably cried, but she was too late. The hour of grace she denied. This is enough now. Tomorrow we shall come again, and see more souls that are sealed under satanic reign.

At the great judgement, for the names that are not written in the Book of Life, the second death is imminent. Friends of sin, be born again. With all your heart seek the Lord. Wake up before it is too late, and stand on His Holy Word. Hell is so real, and there is no way out of that evil place. Jesus is Love; He will forgive and protect you by His grace.

I could not eat or sleep. All I could see was Hell. To a blind, deaf world, how could I these frightful things tell? Hell is for Satan and his angels for eternity. He blinds people to God's saving grace that can set them free. Jesus came again, "Don't be afraid. Follow Me, I am with you. All is well. Tonight we are going to visit the right leg of Hell."

I cringed in the atmosphere of decayed flesh and agonized cries. Demons and imps growled as they passed us by. Tenderness and love Jesus' face did reflect. His sympathy for those who His love did reject. Tears of compassion ran down His cheeks: "Remember, dear child, the words that I speak. Sometimes it will seem I will be far away, but I never will leave you. I am your constant stay. You must be tempered for what lies ahead, to prepare you to bring this message to the living dead."

We walked along the path that was burned and dry, as screams filled the air. The repugnant smell of death and darkness was everywhere. There was no end to the flaming pits that I could see. I felt so sick and weak, but Jesus strengthened me.

Another woman we stopped to see, had been very popular because of riches, charm and beauty. Satan captured and deceived her by his fraud. She began to love him and spurned the love of God.

The demon spirits were horrifying to see. One was like a big brown grizzly. Some like bats, monkeys, cats, and rats; some were like a horse with smooth skin; but all were most terrifying. Jesus said,"Watch, listen and you will see, the method of their attacks and evil strategy.

Satan said, "Go, do all the evils you possibly can! Destroy homes and families; Seduce the weak Christian!" Away they went through a funnel to a blind world to carry out the cruel, wicked plans of Satan. They smelled like Satan, and invisibly they went to claim a host of humanity to populate Satan's hellish domain.

"This place is filled with those who had known the way. They loved the world, flesh and the devil, so fleshly living they did display. It would have been much better if Me they had not received, than to turn again to the love of sin, and not believe." It was the same in the many pits we passed by. When Jesus couldn't help them they raged, cursed, and cried! It made me so sick I could hardly stand. Jesus so sweetly strengthened me again, and held my hand.

"This man was killed in a crash at twenty-three. He was brought up in a church, but wouldn't listen to Me. He loves sex, drinks, drugs and sinful partying, so the fruit of his flesh he is now receiving." His cries of shameful regret inside me rang for days.

Young people, dear young people, turn from your sinful ways! This world and all that is in it shall soon be gone forever, but God's word shall not pass away; never, not ever! The reality of Hell is far worse than I could imagine. Are friends and relatives, there, paying the price of sin?

Jesus said, "Tell them to shun Hell at all cost! They must repent of their sin or be inevitably lost! They have My sympathy, I know how they feel, but because of their choice I couldn't save or heal. All of their sin and judgement on Me was laid, so My life blessing could in them be portrayed.

I was shocked when the next case was revealed to me. A woman was saved, prayed and preached holiness faithfully. She heard her husband with another woman did go. Her heart hardened with bitterness. She hated him so. He deeply repented and begged her to forgive. She stoutly refused and in bitterness lived, until she shot them both and herself, too.

"Oh please let me out! I'll preach forgiveness everywhere I go! I'll tell them the price of an unforgiving spirit! I'll make people know!" "You hardened your heart, but had this realization. I came to you, not in condemnation, but with Salvation. I sent many to help you to forgive, but in your bitterness, you determined to live. There is no anger or bitterness worth going to Hell for -- the degree of punishment you will have to endure. My grace is sufficient for you to forgive. I love to forgive you so you could in blessing live."

Backslidden preachers and backsliders were imprisoned here. A big preacher said, "God is Love. We have nothing to fear! We can enjoy our sin. I don't believe Hell is real! Satan told me to preach this so my soul in Hell he could seal! I know there are many souls I have led astray. "Yes," said Jesus, "I tried to stop you, but you went your way. It is too late now, for eternity you will regret. You know God's word is true, and His judgement is set."

In the Earth all the abominations God hates are there. Evil forces are ushering millions to their pits of despair. The whole world, God with his broom of destruction is sweeping. He's making a speedy riddance of sin. This is His last cleansing.

Another woman said, "I was a good church member. I knew I had a call on my life, I wanted to obey, I remember." "Woman, you are full of lies and sin. You would not listen to Me. You enjoyed gossiping, a double life and a double tongue. You're here for eternity."

We came through the ghastly tunnel of fear into the belly of Hell. There was a four foot walk in front that was full of barred cells. Whatever they had in the world did not help them here. All were bony dark skeletons in suffering and pain, haunted by fear.

There was a coffin -- twelve demons around it were walking, piercing the soul within with sharp spears, who in agony was crying. Jesus told me to look inside. I cried: "How could that soul still have life?"

216

"Satan put him here. Torturing him like this is his delight."
"He had been a preacher but had committed the
unpardonable sin, so for him there was no forgiveness. The
baptism of the Spirit and speaking in tongues he denied, and
turned aside those whom on his preaching relied."

I followed the Lord around the walkway before the cells. I
looked down on the dimly lit centre of Hell. There was the
greatest amount of Hell's activity. Many forms were moving
about, surrounded by cells as far as I could see. Souls here
delighted in wickedness. Evil sin was their love and passion.
Against God they worked the greatest abominations. Satan
administers different torments.

The Day of Judgment will come at last. Then Death and Hell
into the Lake of Fire shall be cast. The Lord hadn't yet let
me hear the volume of cries that from their cells came. I was
shocked: Those emaciated bodies, their mind could retain.

For a poor woman my heart ached and for her I lamented.
She was terrified: a bear unlocked her cell and dragged her
to Satan to be tormented. "She chose to live wickedly, her
life to Satan willingly gave. Because of her choice My
compassion and mercy could not save. My heart aches for
the agony of her eternal fate. Her sin and punishment I bore
for her but now her repentance was too late."

As far as I could see those cells were in a circle without end.
I could hear moans, groans wails and sighs, without a friend.
Jesus said, "They preached for Satan, a counterfeit ministry.
The inevitable reward is this Hell for eternity.

Satan still thinks he can overthrow God and disrupt His plan
but he was defeated when I bore the sin of the world for
man. His sentence is written. His judgement is set. For his
love to lie, cheat, torture, kill and destroy, he too will regret.

You must sincerely give your heart to God and serve Him
alone. I'm about to reveal a horrible reality to you. Your
soul shall groan. It must be so the world can hear, the
reality of the Hell they will have to bear.

217

All these things are being indelibly written on your heart, without a doubt so that Hell's reality can not be forgotten, or rationalized out. Many shall repent and give their life to Me, because of this clear vision I now give thee." Jesus told me there was a place in Hell called the Fun Centre. Although torments differ for souls, all are burned with fire. Satan made his circus like an arena for his entertainment; here he has made every method for torture and torment. One is a demonic scavenger hunt Satan designed. Spiritual bones are torn apart and hid for the demons to find. The poor souls cry for death, but find no rest. Satan ordered all this done for his entertainment. This is how he has fun.

"One time these cells were in Paradise but when I died, I moved Paradise. Satan then took this over for his vice. He is ever enlarging it to have room to receive, the multitudes he has bound, robbed and deceived. In their agony they had to worship, praise and bow to him, so very great is his lust for adoration. If only they had listened and turned to Me, I would have broken their chains and set them free."

I saw a black object the size of a big baseball diamond. "This is the heart of Hell; see it is moving up and down. Those branches are pipes to spew out evil on all nations, to bring forth the Antichrist who will turn many from Salvation. Evil kingdoms shall bring forth the beast, then many from Me shall depart. It all had its beginning in this wicked, evil heart."

We walked up some stairs, a door opened and we went in. I could hardly breathe. It was totally dark. Suddenly Jesus was gone. The shock I couldn't believe. "Jesus, where are You?" I wailed, "Come and take me home!" It was here I really experienced Hell's sorrow and doom. In the darkness, grief and fear, I saw I was not alone. There was a yellow light; two big demons with a chain had come. They wrapped me in it and dragged me deep into the heart. "Jesus! Jesus! Please come and take my part!" They laughed sarcastically, "Jesus let you down. He went away." They pushed me into a cell and said, "That's where you stay!"

218

"Why am I here? What is wrong?" I cried to no avail.
I realized I was lost; lost in the heart of Hell. In intense
loneliness and utter despair, I cried. It was so bad. A
woman in the next cell said, "No use to pray. There is no
help to be had! Satan will come and torture us for his
pleasure. The agony then is beyond measure. I was a
prostitute. My life was filled with sin and misery. Many
have made their bed in Hell because of me. I can't forget the
sin that brought me here. I am in constant agony and
ghastly fear. To the horrors I have to suffer there is no end.
I wish I had accepted the Lord as my Saviour and Friend."

"But, I {Mary} am saved, I belong to God! Why am I here?
Why? Jesus please help me. Dear Lord, let me die!" My
echo was the only reply. "Lord Jesus where are you! Please
help me out! Why did this happen? What brought it about?"

Demons came and dragged me through dirt to Satan's altar,
and to him made me bow. Satan gave a fiendish laugh, "No
Jesus here! I'm your king now!" I recoiled in horror with an
awful realization; I was completely helpless in this doomed
situation. "Take her to the deepest part of the heart. All
horrors pour until she learns she belongs to me and calls me
her Lord." Obediently they dragged me to a deep, dark, cold
and clammy cell. I was cold and burning at the same time;
and saturated with that horrifying smell. Excruciating pain
swept over me. I hurt beyond belief. "Jesus, please come! I
belong to you and I'm in such grief!"

At once light filled that place. Jesus held me in His loving
arms. Instantly we were standing back in my home. "Lord,
where were you? Why did you leave me in the heart of Hell?"
"My child, I had to let you go through this so you could tell,
without a shadow of a doubt the reality of Hell. I was with
you in all that suffering. I love you, My child!"

I didn't think I could ever be normal again. In His mercy He
completely restored me and healed the pain. He gave me
the strength to go with Him back into that place. There was
much more to teach and show of His all sufficient grace.

I couldn't believe it -- something so pretty in Hell: Five beautiful women so charming they seemed unreal. Jesus told me to watch; it was very fascinating. Elaborately dressed on an admirable floor, to music they were dancing. Sweetly they sang, "Hail Satan! Hail!"

Satan gloated over their praise; but he had a message to tell, "My daughters, you have obeyed me and done well my will. I'm sending you back to Earth my plan to fulfil. To impress on you, you must obey me explicitly, my power will show you my tormenting reality." "Oh please, please don't! We'll listen and do what you say." Satan laughed, "You are to experience it anyway!"

I was shocked, instead of their exquisite comeliness, instantly they changed to the dead flesh of Hell, loathsome in ugliness. "Lord Satan, give us back our beautiful bodies!" They all cried out, but they fell apart and hideous snakes from their insides crawled about. Satan laughed at their pain but waved his arms and their charm returned. "Now go!" Act like normal people! Don't let anyone know! The aim of your mission is to turn people from God to me. I'll be watching you. All Hell is behind you, your strength and cunning to be." Screens showed them in towns, schools, churches and bars; their work was underhand. Satan laughed, "They are doing a great job accomplishing my plan! They will bring in a great host for my glory and reign. Their reward will be a Hell of misery and pain."

If they do not choose to serve the Lord they will serve the devil. Many good men are captured by his evil. We stopped before a group of demons who were singing and praising. Jesus said He would let me know what they were saying:

"We will go to this house to destroy those that are there, with sickness, pain and misery, take away their desire for prayer. We will break up home and family, and seduce the weak Christian." They worshipped Satan with their song and dance, and delighted in their evil chants. "We must be aware of those who know the power of Jesus' name. They will cast us out and cause us much pain."

220

Jesus said, "My angels protect My people and bind the demonic hands. I have many angels employed to stop Satan's diabolical plans. I am preparing My holy army to do My will. Men, women, boys and girls My purpose shall fulfil. They will serve Me with all their heart and I will bless them with boldness, in the Spirit of Holiness. Many will be surprised at those whom I have chosen, to do exploits for Me according to My pattern. I've searched for them in city, country and town; My all seeing eye will not miss one.

"Lord Jesus, I want to be worthy to be in Your army. I know I must be like You, pure and holy. I know you will have to break this house of clay, to bring forth Your fruits of righteousness abundantly.

"Tonight we will visit the right arm of Hell." In it were no pits, but a fiery river. Satan made a great wind to blow, it seemed everything it would devour. In it were multitudes of skeletons -- men with men, women with women chained together. What they loved on earth they hated now, and would forever. Many boys and girls they dragged into misery and sin. For their guilt and their crimes is this great suffering. God is a God of justice. They reap what they sow. Being bound together with a chain is a reminding goad.

Things shall quickly take place. Evil is rampant in these last days. Men are lovers of themselves instead of God, and will now pass under the judgment rod.

Jesus said, "We are through. I will not show you all of Hell, but what has been revealed be faithful and tell. We will go now into the jaws of Hell. A loud noise! Jaws opened! Lost souls screamed as they fell! Then the ghastliness that I felt before. Jesus had gone. He had gone for sure. "Oh no! Not again!" I cried, "Not again! Jesus don't leave me in this awful strain!"

I ran down the hill crying for Jesus to help me. A demon said, "He let you down. He went away. You're here to stay!" "Let me go! Let me go!" I frantically cried! "Nowhere to go! This is your eternal abode!" He sneered.

221

A stinking film spread over me. My body was in a state of decay. The worms so abundant, I couldn't drive them away. An ugly rat bit me on the leg. In desperation I cried! "Jesus, where are you? Please let me die!" There was no reply. I was hungrier and thirstier than ever I had been. I knew everything. The pain tore me persistently. There was weeping, gnashing of teeth and hopelessness. I knew I was in the place of outer darkness.

"How do I get out? What is ahead? Oh Lord, where are you? Help me!" I pleaded. A queen of Satan cursed me and spit in my face, then demonstrated her power. She became a man, a cat, a horse, a snake and a rat with evil laughter. Two hours went by. Often I heard that loud sound and souls falling into Hell. My body suffering horrible changes, my mind was clear as a bell. I began to sing about the Blood of Jesus which is able to save from sin. I prayed for the people on Earth, "Lord, please save them!"

"Stop it!" Screamed large demons who with spears came and stabbed me. Hot flashes of fire pierced me again and again. Moans and groans filled the filthy air, and mine joined with them in their cries of despair. I fell in a heap, feeling the torments. New pain came. I had prayed for the sick and they were healed in Jesus' Name. I remembered His wonderful words of love, His faithfulness. I thought: "I would not be here if I had been more like Jesus."

All at once I was lifted from that cell by an unseen force. When I regained consciousness, we were standing by my house. "Why Lord? Why?" I fell at His feet and despair filled my soul. "Peace be still." He lifted me tenderly in His arms and said: "I am in control." I fell asleep in His arms. When I awakened, I was sick and in shock for many a day. I knew what the lost went through when they went to Hell to stay. I completely recovered; my spirit Jesus made whole. The sweetness of His presence filled my soul. Jesus told me I was born and called this message to tell, of the agonies of the lost and how to escape Hell. These facts are indelibly written on my soul today. I can't forget them, and you can't take them away.

222

"If you are a Christian be sure your heart is clean. I don't want you to see the place where twice I've been. In all your tests keep your eyes on Jesus. He'll strengthen you. In the anointing of His Spirit, do what He wants you to do.

I'm grateful to Jesus for complete recovery and healing at last. His wonderful presence strengthened me for this difficult task. The recorded scriptures in the back of the book confirm the message is true. Use your Bible as you read and know this is God's Word to you.

I am still overwhelmed by my husband's confidence in me. The love of my children and help of Godly friends as this book became reality. It was a long suffering period before this project came to an end. I praise the Lord for God-given helpers and Jesus my loving, faithful Friend."

This poem on Mary Kathryn Baxter's Visit to Hell does not do justice to the book. I have gleaned some of her revelations and experiences, and woven them into a poem to give a poetical word picture of Hell. My ways of expression are not just like Mary's, but the truth expressed is the same. When I could, I used her words.

We know there is a God. We know there is a Satan. We know there is a Heaven, and just as assuredly there is a Hell. There is Heavenly bliss for the faithful and true and all unbelievers will have to go to the devil's Hell.

I treasure her book. It not only confirms many things I felt, but it is a door of revelation that lets the light shine on my vague conceptions.

I have never had the privilege of meeting Mary Kathryn Baxter. Maybe the Lord will cross our paths some day. Her initials are the same as mine. Our burdens are the same. I am happy to help her herald this message in any way that I can. It has intensified my burden in prayer. I thank you, Mary. May the Lord fulfil His great mercies in you and keep you in the hour of temptation. Amen.

The Prevailing Bride

The Bride is not defeated; against all Hell She shall prevail.
She'll win through holiness, power, the word, and travail. 1
Be in the stature and fullness of Christ, Ephesians declares.
The Lord's mighty works were fulfilled by fasting and prayer.
He adopted and ordained us to be His representation,
All He did shall be brought forth in glorious manifestation.
Just as He was the exact image of His Father in Heaven
So shall we be according to the word He has given.

He took all of our judgement so He could give us all of Him;
Thus a wonderful organic union He ushered in.
Heavenly genes and culture replace our carnality,
And from the corruption of the flesh, we are free.
The difference between the Bride and the Church today
Is that She listens intently to what Jesus has to say.
He has given us all power and authority through His name,
So that the works He did, we will do the same.

We'll hate the wickedness of our godless carnality,
And desperately cry for His purity, righteousness and reality.
We are coming through hot fire, realizing our sinful state.
We are changed into His likeness, of which is no duplicate.
Jeremiah 6 says the spoiler comes quickly, fast and repent.
Zephaniah 3 says: God's people will serve with one consent.
Seek righteousness and meekness. In Him abide 2
To be worthy to escape His wrath, with whom He'll hide.

We must know who we are in Christ and be one with the Jew.
God'll make us a praise among all people as He said He'd do
We can change the history of nations. Hold the enemy at bay,
And bring forth those appointed to Salvation, if we will obey.
Today God's terrors are round about; 3
None shall escape; man will have no way out.
Every man shall be salted with fire; 4
This refining, we shall certainly require. 5

---

1. Ephesians 4:13   2. Zephaniah 2:3
3. Lamentations 2:22   4. Mark 9:41   5. Zechariah 13:9